Friends
the Hospital

SENIOR nurses enjoy the League's summer fete in the 1960s, among them
Sisters Challen, Taylor, Lampard, Langer, Foulkes and Jarvis.

**A history of volunteering at Horsham Hospital
marking the 50th anniversary of
The League of Friends of Horsham Hospital,
February 27, 2009**

Written and compiled by David Briffett

Friends of the Hospital

Friends of the Hospital

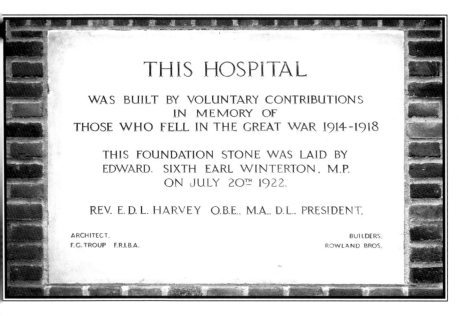

THIS HOSPITAL

WAS BUILT BY VOLUNTARY CONTRIBUTIONS
IN MEMORY OF
THOSE WHO FELL IN THE GREAT WAR 1914-1918

THIS FOUNDATION STONE WAS LAID BY
EDWARD. SIXTH EARL WINTERTON, M.P.
ON JULY 20TH 1922.

REV. E. D. L. HARVEY O.B.E., M.A., D.L., PRESIDENT.

ARCHITECT.
F.G.TROUP   F.R.I.B.A.

BUILDERS.
ROWLAND BROS.

LIST OF CONTENTS

IN MEMORY OF CO-FOUNDER MOLLY ANDREWS

'Friends of the Hospital' is dedicated to the memory of Molly Andrews, co-founder of the League who devoted 36 years of her life to the well-being of the hospital between 1944 and 1980. This history is published by the League of Friends of Horsham Hospital, with a contribution from donations made in Molly's memory, and all proceeds will be devoted to hospital activities

The League and volunteers will always be needed

MY sincerest congratulations to all the many people who have been associated with The League of Friends during the past fifty years.

Your record is truly outstanding and I am proud that my family has been closely associated with your many activities for all of this time. My mother Lavinia became Patron in the founding year of 1959 and held that office for 36 years until her death when I happily accepted the great honour of succeeding her.

It is fitting that there should be a written record of the amazing voluntary work that has been so prominent in the life at Horsham Hospital ever since the first buildings went up in 1892, and I am sure that this booklet will provide future generations with an invaluable history as well as providing a much deserved tribute to the numerous people responsible for a remarkable era of fund raising.

The shape of the health service continues to change year by year, but there is one thing we can be very sure about: the League of Friends and its many volunteers will always be needed.

The Lady Mary Mumford,
Patron, League of Friends of Horsham Hospital

Bonds that link 1892 with 2009

THIS booklet is dedicated to the history of the League of Friends of Horsham Hospital and its remarkable first 50 years. It is also a story of volunteering in Horsham through many generations and a tribute to the legions of people who have come forward during the past century or more to freely give their time to the life of the hospital.

It is not possible to identify all those who have taken part in this great adventure, nevertheless a few names stand out.

People such as the League's co-founder Molly Andrews, a member from its creation in 1959 until her death in 2008. Lavinia, the Duchess of Norfolk, 36 years the League's patron, followed by her daughter The Lady Mary Mumford, who for the past 14 years has continued that support. Founding Chairman Sir John Troutbeck who gave 12 years to the post, and three other chairman Reginald Fisher, Roy Budd and Maggie Parsons who gave nine, twelve and eleven years respectively.

Both Luther Bourne and Leslie Andrews were on the original committee and each devoted more than 30 years to the interests of the League. The energetic Bernard Newman created the Private Members Draw, still running today, and took the League into the recycling business, thereby raising many thousands of pounds. Joan Yarborough launched the first Tea Bar, served three years as Chairman and ran the shop for 14 years. Doug Hartman cherished the shop for more than ten years whilst Val Winterflood became Membership Secretary in 1985 and was still doing the same job 24 years later in our 50th year.

Numerous others have given long and sterling service, unsung heroes behind the scenes who have served teas, worked in the shop, sold books, traded draw tickets, dug over the gardens, organised fund raisers, lugged around bundles of sale items or spent long hours in over heated committee rooms prognosticating and decision making. They are the essence of the volunteering world, unpaid, unrewarded, often unrecognised, yet content knowing that they have done something to help. The community is indebted to them all.

Horsham Hospital exists only because of volunteers and until the year of 1948 was officially classed as a "Voluntary Hospital" before being swallowed up by the National Health Service.

Reading back through old files, I soon realised that you cannot mention the work of hospital volunteers without reference to the inspired people who were responsible for building the hospital in 1892. They raised huge sums of money, received gifts from a generous community and set about supervision of the hospital, raising income to pay the bills, giving up precious time and resources, without seeking or demanding any reward. An age of genuine altruism.

From old hospital records, the considerable research done by former Urban Council Chairman Frank Holmes and the League's very comprehensive file of minutes and annual reports, I have set out to show what miracles have been achieved at Horsham Hospital between 1892 and 2009.

In 1959 the League of Friends took up the mantle left behind by the early pioneers and the common bond between the citizens of 1892 and those who serve today is clear to see. Their accomplishments have been truly remarkable. During the League's first 25 years a sum of £139,946 was spent. This work accelerated year on year until the turn of the century saw volunteers re-equipping both the X-Ray and Minor Injuries departments, helping to create one of the finest Eye Clinics in the region, and donating in a single year the sum of £400,000 boosted by an amazing legacy of £250,000.

In 50 years more than £2 million has been devoted to the well-being of patients, staff and visitors alike. It is an inspirational story of outstanding dedication to a much appreciated institution, a story that is destined to continue.

David Briffett
January, 2009

AUTHOR A JOURNALIST FOR 46 YEARS

David Briffett worked in journalism for 46 years and was Editor of the West Sussex County Times for 24 of them. He is the author of two books about crime and has been actively involved in health service issues for many years. He became a member of the League committee in 2002 and is currently Vice Chairman.

Our thanks

THANKS are due to a number of people who have assisted with the compilation of this booklet including the West Sussex County Times, Horsham Museum, Horsham Hospital staff, former staff, members of the League and others. A special thanks to June Smith, Joy Joy, Reu Brown and Ann Briffett for checking the text and to porter Steve Partlett for his special understanding of hospital history. The photographs have come from a variety of sources, many ancient, and credits are due to West Sussex County Times, Jack Marren, Anthony's Photographers of Horsham, S.A.Ticehurst of Horsham, Springfield Studio of Horsham, Photo Reportage of London and H-B News Features of London, as well as individuals who loaned prints and recounted their memories.

Friends of the Hospital: 1892-1948

Volunteers build and run Hospital for 56 years

THE FIRST 'FRIENDS'

THERE is no doubt that in 1892 Horsham was in desperate need of a hospital. Patients with medical problems in those times were being sent to the County Institution at Brighton, the location of which was described as being "extremely inconvenient".

In the event of a serious accident there was "no place in existence to which the unfortunate sufferer could be taken for immediate assistance", declared the West Sussex County Times.

For poorer members of the community, the prospects of receiving quick medical treatment often relied on charity and the chances of surviving a serious accident or illness were not high. One of the town's most prominent citizens of that era, Charles Lucas of Warnham Park, gave a clear illustration of the dilemma when he said "there could be nothing more sad and touching than to go into the cottages of the poor and find the head of the family on a bed of sickness huddled together with his family without the necessities and comforts needed for his recovery."

A report issued by the Local Board of Health in 1891 listed the deaths of 30 children under the age of one and recorded a smallpox epidemic which, in the absence of a hospital or place of isolation, resulted in all cases being treated in tents in a field adjacent to the Workhouse.

This lack of available care had been apparent to many residents for some 25 years whilst several attempts to provide a hospital had proved ineffectual. The man who stepped up to resolve the issue was the Vicar of Horsham, the Reverend Charles J.Robinson, who had become so concerned about the cramped and insanitary conditions in which many people lived that he put out a rallying call for action.

The Vicar's predecessors could claim a long tradition of providing succour for the sick stretching back many centuries. In medieval times there had been a hospice in Normandy adjacent to the parish church of St.Mary; at around 1600 it had become a poorhouse run by the parish and from 1842 converted to almshouses, known as St.Mary's Hospital.

The almshouses opened when inmates of the old poorhouse were transferred to a new Union Workhouse in Crawley Road, Roffey, around the year 1838, a building that had its own infirmary, served as a military hospital during the Second World War and thereafter became known as Forest Hospital.

The Reverend Robinson declared his intention to raise money as a matter of urgency to provide the town with a desperately needed hospital, designed to serve ordinary folk and especially the poor. He was the inspiration, he was the first "friend" and it must be said that dozens of people flocked to his call, including many of the wealthy land-owning class of the times who, along with their wives, became avidly devoted to the cause.

A public meeting at Horsham Town Hall on December 15, 1890, resulted in £963 being pledged with immediate effect and the setting up of a committee of town worthies who "recognised the advantage which would be conferred on Horsham and the neighbourhood by the establishment of a Cottage Hospital" and who forthwith pledged themselves to offer "cordial support" towards such a scheme. Most important of all, the Hurst family of Park House offered a piece of land for the building, free of charge.

The vicar's main supporters on that historic day were C.R.Scrase Dickens, E.I.Bostock, the Rev.R.A.C.Bevan, Edward Henty, C.T.Lucas and F.W.Pigott. Others rallied around them and the first general committee contained no fewer than 48 citizens, all men, whose names were neatly recorded in the minutes: Sir Prescott Hewell, Messrs Walford, C.T.Lucas, C.J.Lucas, Harben, Cattley, J.D.Godman, P.S.Godman, Hubbard, Dickins, Bostock, Kinneir, Hurst, Allcard, Pigott, Laideman, Attree, Seth Smith, Whitaker, Brown, Christy, Michell, Innes, Lintott, Stott, Hunt, Sewell, Bethune, Gallier, Coleman, Oddie, Churchman, Price, Rawlinson, Sadler, Brooks, Padwick, Colonel Smith, Colonel John and the Reverends Masters, Munro, McCarogher, Bowcott, Frost, Hugesson, Willis, Taylor and Robinson.

Many of these names still echo around Horsham today.

So top heavy was this "committee" that a more streamlined executive committee was required and this they boiled down to 13, Scrase Dickens, appointed Chairman, sitting alongside Messers Pigott, C.T.Lucas, Cattley, Bostock, Harben, Kinneir, Allcard, P.S.Godman, Stott, Hunt, Colonel Smith and the good promoter himself the Rev.Robinson.

What they began, others built upon. The Hurst family who gave up precious lands for building and subsequent expansion, the Allcard family who gave much time, energy and hard cash, the Reverend Harvey who led the way for a second and larger hospital, and the likes of Mick Cope, caretaker and porter for 35 years, the latter three having been remembered in the names of wards which endured for generations.

They all deserve our thanks for the emergence of Horsham Hospital for it is they who lit a spark which continues to bring forth health service volunteers to this day.

HOW DID THEY DO IT ?

THE support for a hospital during 1891 was overwhelming. Only seven months after the formation of the committee they had succeeded in raising all the money required, a quote from a builder had been accepted and construction work was underway.

By the February of that year the donation tally had risen to £1,308 along with promises of annual subscriptions amounting to £141, essential for running costs. A list of donors was published regularly in the West Sussex County Times, thus helping to spur things along. Typical of the benefactors who came forward was Mr. Eversfield who stumped up a lump sum of £100 and pledged another £5 per year.

The catalyst that made all things possible was the Hurst family's offer of land. The Hursts had been prominent in the district for centuries having provided several MPs from amongst their ranks as well as owning large tracts of land around the town, including Park House in North Street and its extensive parkland.

Mr.R.N.Hurst had noticed the campaign, he must have personally known several members of the first committee and made it his public duty to come forward to say that he was prepared to donate a site for a new hospital. Three members of the committee met him and together they looked at three different Horsham sites, one in Crawley

Road and the other two in Hurst Road itself, one on the north side and the other on the south side.

This was a chance too good to miss and the sub-committee wasted little time inspecting each site, promptly recommending to their colleagues land to the north of Hurst Road, a site where Horsham Art School was later established. At a meeting on February 20, 1891, the main committee accepted the gift, however soon afterwards Mr.Hurst came up with a fourth alternative, a larger plot to the south of Hurst Road opposite the junction with Richmond Road and upon which were two cottages, both available for purchase.

These committee men of a past century were nothing if not flexible. Another meeting was hastily called for March 5 during which the first decision was rescinded and amicable agreement was obtained to accept the fourth land option, so generously given by the Hursts, added to which they would pay a sum of £200 to secure the two cottages, both useful buildings that could be adapted for various purposes.

With land now secured and more money flowing in, there must have been a real buzz of excitement amongst these pioneers as they appointed a firm of architects to draw up plans for the hospital. By modern standards this was not going to be a huge building, however for the community of Horsham it was a ground-breaking development. The provision was for eight beds with rooms for tackling emergencies, carrying out surgical work and accommodation for Matron with a very small staff.

The plans were first examined by the committee on May 22 and by June 5 they had received full approval. Local builders were given until July 25 to place tenders for the work and six bids were received by deadline day with estimates ranging from £1,289 up to £1,680. The committee selected the lowest bidder Rowland Brothers who were asked to provide a verandah to the building at a cost not exceeding £11, thus bringing the total contract price up to £1,300. The deal was done.

JULY 1892: THE COTTAGE HOSPITAL OPENS

IT was a very proud moment for the committee and its many supporters when they erected a board at the Hurst Road building site announcing "Horsham Cottage Hospital, supported by voluntary contributions."

Designed by Horsham architect Frederick Wheeler with a cottage-style interior that combined "neatness with compactness", the interior boasted "every provision for modern hospital requirements". A wide staircase led to wards on the first floor with three beds for men, three for women and two others alongside a surgery, operating room, bathroom, cupboards and a nurses' room. Ground level provided waiting room, an "urgency ward" which undoubtedly was the forerunner of a Casualty Department, medical stores and various rooms for Matron, nurses and servants. Gardens at the rear measuring 80 feet by 200 feet were tastefully laid out, accommodating a laundry and a mortuary.

Just one year and six months after the first public meeting the new hospital was built and ready to function. "An institution destined to perform a noble work amongst the suffering of the town and neighbouring parishes opened at Horsham on Saturday afternoon," reported the County Times. "Through the liberality of leading residents it will supply a want that has long existed."

THE Cottage Hospital built in 1892 at a cost of £1,300 was paid for and run by volunteers for many years. The building has done sterling service in many different guises and remains part of the health service today.

Painting by Alan Snelling, former maintenance supervisor at the hospital

The ceremony was performed on July 2, 1892 at 3pm by the newly elected President of the management committee, Charles T.Lucas, duly promoted from amongst the ranks of the launch team. He praised the choice of site on the border of Horsham Park in a secluded part of town providing a large rear garden. He had been delighted by the overwhelming success of the public appeal and believed that the hospital would provide lasting benefit to the sick and needy of Horsham providing "every comfort, plain and simple food, fresh air and attention."

The deeds of the building were ceremoniously handed over to four Trustees, Reginald Hurst, Charles Scrase-Dickins, F.W.Pigott and Charles J.Lucas.

Most importantly of all, it was announced that sufficient money was at hand to pay for the entire cost of the project put at £1,950. Of this, £1,289 went to the builder, £200 for the cottages, £55 to the architect, £56 for landscaping the grounds and £350 for furniture and equipment. It was estimated that the annual running costs would be £40 for each bed, thus a sum of £320 would need to be raised each year, money that would come from subscriptions, collections made in churches and chapels and other donations.

The 1895 balance sheet showed running costs of £365 and income of £370 made up of £91in gifts, £218 subscriptions, £52 patient fees and £9 interest. In due course an endowment fund was established by investing in stocks which yielded annual income.

More significant decisions followed. A Ladies Committee drawn from many of the town's leading women of that time was established, including Mrs.Allcard, Mrs. Scrase Dickens, Mrs.Hurst, Mrs.Lintott, Mrs.Lucas and Mrs.Robinson whose initial duties were to supervise the hospital's domestic arrangements, however there can be little doubt that these public spirited ladies set in motion the fund raising work that ultimately would be essential to paying annual running costs which, as years went by, began to increase significantly.

The only person on the fulltime payroll was the first matron, Miss Edith Harrison who came with good credentials from the Westminster Hospital in London, though she had the help of a "ward maid". The medical staff of five consisted E.I.Bostock, F.W.E. Kinneir, F.A.Dukes, T.Kirsopp and H.H.Vernon, all duly registered and legally qualified practitioners resident in the town and who offered their services free of charge.

The committee gave them entire control over the medical affairs of the hospital and it was arranged that one should act as Medical Officer for a week in rotation with powers to ensure the well-being of all patients. In 1897 Horsham police asked if they could borrow stretchers in emergencies, but were told firmly no.

There were 23 clauses in the Hospital Rule Book, some of them pretty strict, and the committee had 1,000 copies printed at a cost of £4.15.6d. No one was allowed in without a Letter of Recommendation from a respected person "duly filled up in all particulars", though emergencies were excepted, and completely banned were people afflicted with any disease considered to be infectious or contagious, or those with epilepsy, insanity, or any disorder "not likely to be soon cured or mitigated by treatment." Also on the banned list: women advanced in pregnancy.

The only exceptions were cases of serious accident or sudden emergency, but even in these cases applications were expected, presumably because there were only eight beds available at any one time. Hospital staff were responsible for providing "decent clothing" and changes of linen for all patients, "except in cases of emergency". The maximum stay was two months.

Most importantly, it was decided that each patient should pay a weekly cash contribution fixed by the committee at somewhere between a minimum of 2s.6d. and a maximum of 10s.6d, though the committee wisely gave themselves power to remit the whole or part of any such contribution at their discretion in cases of genuine hardship. This money would have been of vital help in purchasing incidentals for the hospital, though it was clearly nowhere near sufficient to run the enterprise. Matron was given the task of sending out the bills and collecting the cash.

The Horsham Cottage Hospital was, de facto, a voluntary run organisation, dependent almost entirely on the goodwill of the community.

During its first year 62 patients were admitted, 37 surgical and 25 medical, with 34 coming from the town and the remainder from villages, resulting in many messages of grateful thanks. The first patient record book, which miraculously survived a hospital fire, covers in precise detail the treatments given to patients between 1892 and 1909, how they fared and what fees they were charged.

The very first patient was sixteen year-old Rose Field from Slinfold who spent 38 days receiving treatment given by Dr.Vernon for a hip joint problem, had the condition "relieved" and paid a bill for £1.10s. All manner of illnesses were treated and many operations carried out including amputations, removal of tumours, vast numbers of tonsils and adenoid removals for children, gastric ulcer treatments and care for accident victims including those with gunshot wounds.

Only a few patients actually died, most having been "cured", "relieved" or "improved" during those first 17 years.

COMMUNITY MEETS ANNUAL RUNNING COSTS

THE running of Horsham Hospital remained in the hands of the voluntary management committee for many years and its income stemmed directly from the people of the town and villages who responded with great generosity.

At first the annual subscriptions and donations from regular supporters was enough, however as time went by it became increasingly necessary to run special fund raising events and this is where the Ladies Committee really did come up trumps.

It is not too difficult to conjure up a vision of the town's prominent wives endlessly indulging in new and enterprising schemes whilst their equally illustrious menfolk would meet over lunch to decide how that money would be invested and then how it would be utilised to pay the hospital's weekly bills. What cannot be denied is that this system worked very effectively for many years and that the town's population was never shy in giving a few pounds to the hospital cause.

Church congregations of all denominations were regular contributors whilst groups of railway workers, policemen, postmen, working men's clubs, building firms and hotel owners chipped in money on a regular basis. People organising regular social events would readily part with some of their proceeds including such as Horsham District Football Association, Lower Beeding Stoolball Club, Horsham Football Club and Southwater Church of England Missionary Society. The donations were often small, but when placed together made a significant contribution.

Frank Holmes reveals the 1910 story of how Horsham Football Association offered a £2 donation in return for being granted a free bed to any footballer or deserving case recommended by them. The committee firmly said no then, however a few years later they did enter into a special deal which involved the Association making a £40 donation for which free treatment would be provided for two injured players each season.

Thousands of individual contributions were received over the years as people from all walks of life gave a thought to their precious new hospital. Most of these payments were recorded in the minutes of management committee meetings and this short summary covering a seven year flashback gives some idea of what went on: League of Mercy £563, Billingshurst Bonfire Society £52, Brook Farm Geese £87, Smiths Charity £100, Lady Loder's Gardens £224, Horsham Amalgamated Friendly Societies £112, Old Collyerians Association Dances £106, Whist Drives £40, Charity Cup football £122, Cricket Club £10, Police Ball £104, Billingshurst Hospital Letters Fund £46, Mrs Latilla Tennis Exhibition £139.

Later in the 1930s Horsham Justices imposed a levy on Sunday ticket sales at three town cinemas enabling annual grants to be made to the hospital.

It was upon such generosity that the hospital continued to flourish. However, the organising of finances did not always go smoothly and after the initial wave of enthusiasm there was an apparent decline in income which resulted in a series of deficits and new public appeals had to be launched. One of the worst moments came in 1911 when for the first time precious reserves had to be used to clear debts, payment of gas bills were deferred and requests made to the bank to honour cheques. An appeal in the local paper for monetary help did not work this time and early in 1912 the committee was in the red by £157. It was thanks mainly to a bazaar organised by Mrs.Henderson of Sedgwick Park along with the Ladies Committee that the ship was stabilised with a much needed boost of £125.

There was a continuous need for annual donations and a quest for new enterprises to pay the bills. The ever busy Ladies Committee was responsible for launching what was called "Pound Day", with Miss Allcard taking the lead role, through which people were asked to donate goods in kind and the results for 1929 show that an amazing 698 donors came forward to present the hospital with such items as groceries, meat, eggs, potatoes, butter, fruit, cups and saucers and even boxes of matches. Pound Day became an annual event.

Another of the female inspired enterprises involved the setting up of a Linen Guild which enabled the purchase of many types of linen for hospital use at discounted prices, including sheets, table cloths, dressing gowns, towelling and tea cloths. The figures for 1929 reveal that £62 was spent on such items but that £7 was deducted from the final bill as discount.

More precious income was derived from grateful residents leaving money in their wills and in the early years 20 legacies produced a sum of £3,921, including the gift of one lady who left, as a final wish, the freehold of four cottages worth £315.

Legacies continue to find their way into the hospital today through the auspices of the League of Friends.

ALLCARD FAMILY STEP IN TO PAY FOR EXPANSION

WITHIN a short period of opening it was realised that the hospital was not large enough to cope with demand as the number of patients needing treatment and operations outstripped the beds available.

It was during 1906 that the first waiting list was begun and the committee began talking about the possibility of enlargement. During 1907 they had drawn up plans for additional beds and once again Rowland Brothers were chosen to undertake the work at a total cost of £492. However, this enterprise was possible only thanks to the generosity of the Allcard family who lived at nearby Wimblehurst.

The Allcards were prominent from the start with Mr.Allcard serving on the launch committee, Mrs.Allcard on the Ladies Committee and Miss Allcard leading the Pound Day campaign. In 1901 the family had come forward with a sum of £321 to help buy a strip of land at the side of the hospital for the construction of a road and alterations to the building which they did in the memory of Mr.Edward Allcard.

On November 1, 1907, a hand written letter from Miss Ethel Allcard informed the main committee that her family would be happy to pay the full amount for the latest scheme to provide more beds and once this work was complete a tablet was erected in the hall as a memorial to Frances Allcard and Frances Edith Allcard.

This expansion met the needs of patients for just a few years, however by 1913 the waiting lists for treatment returned and at the annual meeting of 1916 the President, Mr.P.Chasemore, once more raised the question of hospital enlargement. Many people were in favour of selling off the cottage hospital and to replace it with a more modern building that would provide 25 beds and thus meet the growing needs of the Horsham population.

Of course, they were in the midst of the First World War and little progress could be made at that stage, but the debate had begun.

PIVOTAL ROLE OF THE MATRON

THE life of the hospital revolved around the Matron who in 1894 was being paid the handsome sum of £40 per annum with no other help apart from a "ward maid" who received £12 per annum. At the Christmas of 1898, Matron's pay was boosted to £50 and both the maid and cook received bonuses of ten shillings apiece. On the departure of maid Lizzie Bennett to get married she was awarded a £2 bonus.

By 1904 there had been no further pay rises, but the committee agreed to pay Matron a ten guineas bonus that year and in the next year increased her rate to £60. By the turn of the century it was obvious that the strain on Matron was becoming serious and she was allowed one qualified nurse and a probationer to form the first nursing team. This was increased in 1912 to two qualified nurses who received £30 per annum but no allowances for uniforms. Later another probationer was added because workloads had become "very severe", though her pay was just £10 per year.

Nurses' pay was clearly very poor at that time, yet the accounts reveal that a locum nurse could earn £2.2s. in a week which if multiplied by 52 would have given that person a good deal more than the Matron's annual salary. It is a strange anomaly of the health service that agency nurses seem to fare better than full time staff to this day.

Matron lived in one of the small rooms of the hospital, probably on the lower floor, and in 1900 purchased for her comfort an overmantle, a couch and two chairs. Following a debate in committee over these purchases it was agreed, on the Chairman's casting vote, that they would pay her £2.12.6d for the overmantle since it would be fixed to the wall and thus part of the hospital premises.

In 1906 this over burdened lady reported that one of her patients had developed "alcoholic mania" and asked permission to purchase a strait jacket, handcuffs and manacles for the purpose of restraint.

The life of Matron and her tiny staff was very demanding indeed, though by 1920 her pay had increased to £120 and that of the probationer nurse to £25.

EMERGENCE OF THE PRIVATE PATIENT

FROM the start ordinary patients were required to make modest payments for their hospital stays, however it was soon discovered that additional income could be earned from more wealthy residents who could comfortably afford to pay for all the treatments they received and would willingly pay.

As early as the 1901 annual meeting, speakers raised the question of providing a "private ward" at Horsham with charges of two and a half guineas a week, though the issue was clearly controversial and it was left to the committee to ponder. There were members strongly opposed to the concept, though others saw the benefits that might accrue in terms of revenue for the hospital and possibly the chance for doctors to receive some income from their hospital attendances.

The outcome was that the first private patient was treated by Dr.Vernon in March, 1903, and the committee fixed weekly

charges at £2.2 shillings with extra payments required for operations that required dressings and those cases that needed the attendance of a special nurse. Fees recovered from the first patient amounted to £21.

As private patients became more frequent in 1909 it was decided that payments should be "according to the circumstances of the patient" with a new minimum of three guineas a week in the summer and two and a half guineas in the winter, plus extra charges for a private nurse, special diets, stimulants, medicants, surgical dressings, appliances and for the washing of personal linen. By 1920 the fee had increased to £5.5s a week whilst general ward patients were paying 7s.6d.

The strongest opposition to this trend came from Miss Allcard and her sisters who argued that the hospital was not big enough to accommodate private wards and that these admissions would mean less space for poorer patients. At the 1910 annual meeting they succeeded in having the rules changed so that "all patients shall be medically and surgically treated free except those contracted for by the Friendly Societies". However the debate continued and in 1913 another rule was established that "all patients shall be medically and surgically treated free, except paying patients who, if accommodation permits, may be admitted by special arrangement with the medical staff and committee. Not more than two such patients to be in the hospital at the same time."

With agreed quotas and tighter controls, this was a policy that was to survive for the next ten years.

Hospital records for the first 22 years do not mention payment for the doctors, however from around 1914 they were being allowed to receive fees for the growing number of tonsils and adenoids operations being carried out on children. These operations began placing extra pressures on small hospitals and had resulted from a new regime of medical examinations on all school-children carried out by county council medical officers. Parents were charged five shillings for each operation and at first the hospital was very unsuccessful in collecting the money after the event, so they adopted the policy of payment in advance.

The committee was wholly sympathetic with their Honorary Medical Staff because they did not consider it reasonable for them to take on this additional "national work" without some reward and the change of policy represented a significant shift of emphasis for the doctors.

During the 1920s local authorities were given powers to provide hospitals for the acute sick, however there was no need for Horsham Urban District Council to act because the volunteers had got there first, and were running a very successful enterprise.

NEED FOR A BIGGER HOSPITAL RECOGNISED

THE momentum for a bigger hospital came quickly after the end of the First World War as the volume of patients and operations continued to grow along with another phenomenon, the road traffic accident which began to generate a new list of casualties for hospital staff to handle.

However, whereas the first hospital had been dreamed of and built within one year and six months, the second enterprise would occupy the town's attention for seven years between the first discussions of 1916 and the opening in 1923.

In 1919, the year after the Great War had

concluded, the committee was in discussion with the Horsham War Hospital Supply depot which had ended the hostilities with surplus funds of £1,700 and it was agreed that this could form the nucleus of money to build a new hospital, though it was admitted that a lot more fund raising would have to follow.

Once more the fund raising bandwagon began to roll, architects were brought in and a sub committee began examining likely sites. Committee President of 1920, the Reverend Douglas Harvey, was able to announce that £10,645 had been gathered and two alternative plans had been prepared though there was evident concern about the "enormous costs" entailed. They were looking at a target of £20,000 for a 30 bed hospital.

By 1921 the need for action was greater than ever as waiting lists for beds grew ever longer and in that same year the Rev.Harvey inspired the committee to get cracking, declaring the project to be "a crying need". Many people had donated money as a form of memorial to the tragedies of the First World War and there was no way that he was prepared to let them down. The committee scaled down earlier aspirations and came up with plans for two general wards containing 12 beds each, three private wards, a small casualty section, an X-ray room, accommodation for six nurses, two probationers and four maids on the first floor, plus a laundry and mortuary, at an estimated cost of £13,000.

There were some remarkable parallels with the decisive moves that had led to the first Cottage Hospital in 1892. Apart from the war supply depot windfall, most of the money had come from public donations and there was £12,000 in the bank by 1922. Again it was the Vicar who was the driving force. Once more the Hurst family stepped forward to provide a gift of one and a half acres of land immediately adjacent to the existing hospital with a 330 feet frontage on Hurst Road, ideal for the building. Again it was Rowland Brothers who submitted the lowest tender of £11,786 to win the contract, outbidding the likes of Longley and Son (£12,988) and G.Potter (£13,940).

Full of optimism, that summer they got on with the construction work confident that the greatly increased running costs of the new establishment would continue to be met by the ever faithful public. The Rev.Harvey told members: "The committee feel no alarm on this point as they are confident that the people of Horsham and the neighbourhood will be proud of their new hospital and realising what a great boon it will be to the sick and suffering will see that the necessary funds are forthcoming to keep it going."

The Vicar was so committed to the new hospital plan that he and his family pledged to furnish one whole ward at their own expense, whilst Mr and Miss Allcard came forward to furnish the other. Thus Harvey Ward and Allcard Ward became well known hospital landmarks.

There must have been much relief and satisfaction all round when on Thursday, July 22, 1922, at a small ceremony in Hurst Road, Horsham's MP The Earl Winterton came along to lay the foundation stone.

Even when the financial affairs of this highly ambitious enterprise appeared to be running out of control, the Rev.Harvey and his colleagues held their ground and came up with solutions. As matters turned out, the figure of £13,000 had been seriously under-estimated and at one point the project was £2,000 short, but with the sale of the old Cottage Hospital to Collyer's School for a sum of £2,500, this would be comfortably offset. This transaction proved a tricky one because the original land had been donated by the Hurst family and now it was passing into the hands of the education authority, however the complications were resolved.

In due course the total cost was to exceed £18,500, however the committee had nearly a year in hand before the building would open and during that time they not only managed to find all the money required they also launched a new equipment fund which raised a further £1,271

A truly remarkable fund raising coup and a wonderful achievement.

Impressive hospital entrance as it looked in the 1920's

BUILDING work being completed in 1923 by Rowland Brothers whose sign is still up. On the left, a board reading "Horsham Hospital supported by voluntary contributions"

NEATLY finished front courtyard, which today is the main car park.

1923: NEW HOSPITAL AND A NEW ERA FOR CARE

THE much loved Cottage Hospital closed on May 26, 1923, having given 31 years of sterling service to the community and on June 1 there was a grand opening of the new hospital on an adjacent site performed by Lord Leconfield along with a service of dedication conducted by the Bishop of Lewes. It was proudly announced that the new Horsham Hospital could compare most favourably with any hospital of similar size in the country.

The occasion might have been grander still had not Her Royal Highness Princess Victoria been prevented from attending because of the death of her mother, Her Royal Highness Princess Christian.

The first patients arrived on June 17 and, fittingly perhaps, the first operation was carried out by Dr.Vernon, the senior most member of the medical team who had given many years to the old hospital. It really was a new era for health care in Horsham for the new establishment included an X-ray section under the care of honorary radiographer Mr.Dixon and dental surgery supervised by two honorary dental surgeons, Mr.A.P.Sainsbury and Mr.J.H.Wallace. The Matron then was Miss Birtwhistle who served 25 years between 1913 and 1939

A total of 348 patients were admitted to the general wards in the first year, compared to 63 in 1892, and a total of 277 operations were performed. Within two years a cottage was erected in the grounds to provide for a caretaker and porter, and this is still in use.

It was evident from an early stage that the larger hospital would continue to need voluntary donations to pay for the growing running costs, however it was obvious too that the finances would need to be organised in a much more professional way. The use of private beds became a factor bringing in fees of £491 from 27 patients in the first year, however it was the creation of the Contributory Scheme that proved most important in bringing about financial security and for this purpose a separate committee was established following a public meeting held at Horsham Town Hall.

This concept of asking people to pay regular money towards their local hospital was being introduced around the country and Horsham, which already had a strong tradition of voluntary support begun in 1890, took to it readily. The first committee of 1923 proved very strong and able, consisting: H.Hutton (chairman), F.W.New (secretary),W.G.Brown, W.Child, E.P.Perry, W.P.Peskett, C.E.Pope and A.W.Streeter.

The scheme was quite ingenious. It involved dividing the town into nine districts and the organisation of volunteer collectors whose target was to sign up regular subscribers who would make weekly donations in return for which that person would be entitled to a reduction of fifty per cent in any future hospital fees they might incur, whilst in certain circumstances the treatment would be free. The minimum payment was one penny per week but in reality people gave much more.

During the first year 1,750 contributors donated £283 but by 1930 with expansion into the villages inspired by hard working secretary Mr.New this had grown to 4,000 who gave £1,466 whilst by 1936 there were up to 6,000 members raising a handsome £1,979.

The Contributory Scheme was soon providing a regular £1,200 for the running of the hospital and in time produced surplus funds which in 1936 were used for the purchase of a new wireless system for patients. As this committee worked separately to the main management committee there

BUILT at a cost of £18,500, Horsham Hospital mark two as it appeared soon after the opening in 1923.

THE grand opening ceremony on May 23, 1923, performed by Lord Leconfield and the Bishop of Lewes.

REAR view showing extensive gardens which once provided space for summer fetes and marquee gatherings.

Bird's eye view of hospital and gardens in the 1920's

MEDICAL team and management of 1923. Matron Miss Birtwhistle in all white is accompanied by doctors Sparrow, Bradford, Cruikshank, Kinnier, Vernon, Bostock and Jukes, the final four being survivors of the original 1892 medical staff.

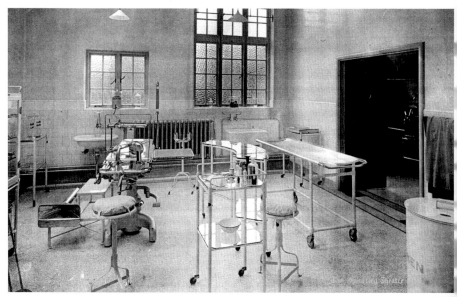

PRISTINE operating theatre in the newly built 1923 building. Many different operations took place, including numerous removals of tonsils, and the department saw more than 80 years of service before decline and final closure.

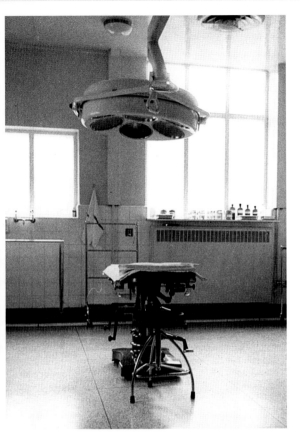

THE operating theatre after major modernisation and lowering of the ceiling, circa 1959. The League stepped in more than once to buy important equipment in order to keep operations going. The site became a new Minor Injuries Unit in 2005.

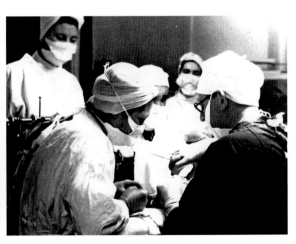

RARE photograph of an operation underway at Horsham in March 1956, performed by Dr.Noel Peach (right) with three nurses and anaesthetist Dr Sidney Morgan.

were sometimes rifts between the two, however their role was much appreciated and the people who ran it were, to all intents and purposes, laying the foundations to be followed much later by today's League of Friends.

The Contributory Scheme had two attractions: the giver was doing something for the wider community but also providing a form of insurance against hospital treatment in the future.

Horsham's very successful scheme kept the hospital going between 1923 and 1948 until the NHS took over.

1930: CHILDREN'S WARD IS A MAJOR ADDITION

FOLLOWING compulsory medical inspection of children in schools, the number of child patients being admitted to the hospital increased dramatically, and it was not just for tonsils. The numbers became so significant that Matron organised Christmas parties for 120 children in 1925 and another 150 in 1926.

Up until now all hospital initiatives had come from the high powered management committee led by its unpaid town worthies. Now there was a change of emphasis. It was the Contributory Scheme committee which passed a resolution calling for the building of a separate 20 bed children's ward for those up to the age of 12.

With its powerful fund raising credentials, the Contributory Scheme committee was in a strong position that could not be denied. The main committee had barely recovered from the immense undertaking of setting up the new hospital when it was faced with this new administrative mountain. However, they happily took the idea on board, identified a suitable site and estimated costs at £5,000.

Fund raising began in earnest and a figure of £1,933 was put together steadily, but the big breakthrough came on Whit Monday of 1929 when Mrs.Latilla raised the enormous sum of £1,873 through a World's Fair held at Marlands, nearly doubling the building fund overnight. This was rapidly followed by £1,000 from Mr.Armitage of Faygate, £500 from Dr.Mosse of Roffey House and a series of smaller donations which meant that the job need be delayed no further.

In that year no fewer than 172 children had passed through the wards and so the argument in favour of a special ward was proven. The original aspiration for 20 beds was cut to ten and builders Bartley and Ward, whose tender of £6,521 was the lowest of three, had the job done by the Autumn of 1930 with the ward being officially opened on December 18 by Lady Leconfield. Workers at The Sussex Brick Company presented two new fully equipped cots and Horsham Chamber of Trade gave a complete wireless set with earphones for each bed.

As in the case of the new hospital, final costs were under-estimated as the bill leapt to £8,000, however true to form the volunteer fund raisers covered every penny and residents became very proud of this facility named Horsham Ward.

One of the rare hospital record books to survive was an inventory carried out in 1934 by estate agents King and Chasemore, undertaken at no cost, which gives a clear illustration of how the hospital was working then. Produced for insurance purposes, it reveals a functioning chapel with candlesticks, crucifix and altar cloths worth £25 and mortuary fittings worth £10, whilst the personal effects of Matron, nurses and servants were put at £500. Matron had an office, sitting room and bedroom, nurses were provided with sitting and dining rooms whilst the servants also had a sitting room and their own hall.

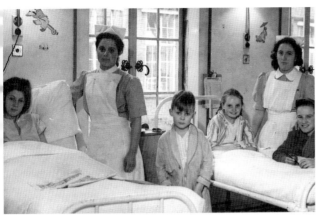

THE CHILDREN'S WARD

THE Children's Ward was established in 1930 at a cost of £6,521 thanks to local fund raising. It was known as Horsham Ward for a time but later re-named Cope Ward after a long serving porter. This photograph was taken in 1949.

ACTIVITIES in the children's day room.

BUSY nurses at work with children during the early 1960s.

Both Harvey and Allcard wards were working with 12 beds each, the Horsham Ward for boys and girls contained ten cots, whilst St.George Ward, St.Andrew Ward and St.Patrick Ward seemed particularly well furnished for single use and were undoubtedly the private wards. There were also a further 17 single bedrooms, though it is not clear from the inventory whether these were for patients or staff.

There were good facilities for operations including a stretcher room, surgeon's room, sterilising room and a fully equipped theatre containing a St.Bart's operating table with all

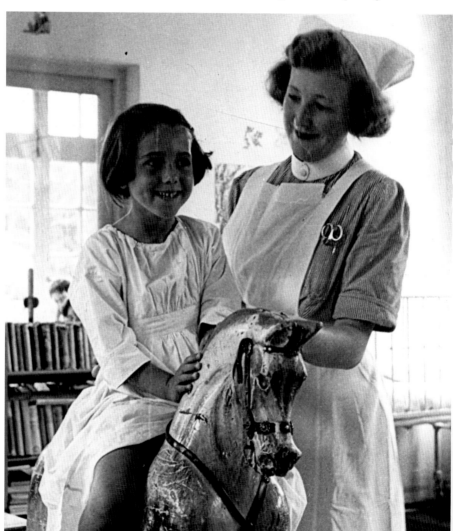

THIS popular rocking horse in the Children's Ward is fondly remembered.

required instruments and anaesthetics. The entire contents of the hospital were valued at £3,795.

The continuing growth of road traffic accidents was putting hospital services under great strain in the 1930s, with 219 such victims handled in 1935, of which many were from outside the area. This resulted in waiting lists for surgery and complications for Matron in retrieving fees from distant insurance firms.

The Reverend Harvey, nine times President of the committee, died in 1938 at the age of 80 and one year later his daughter Mrs.A.T.Hodgson donated £1,000 which, together with £500 from the Contributory Scheme, paid for the establishment of a new X-Ray Department. In the same year another donor presented the hospital with 25,000 bricks, which may well have been used for the building work.

1939-45: THE WAR YEARS HERALD BIG CHANGES

THE First World War had disrupted the life of the hospital and heralded the building of the second hospital. Likewise the chaotic times of the Second World War brought many trials and tribulations and for the first time there was an element of Government involvement in its running, a precursor to the later arrival of the NHS.

As part of the national war plan, Horsham Hospital was placed under the command of an officer of the Ministry of Health, staff members were issued with Ministry badges and there were instructions for co-ordination with the military hospital established in the former Horsham Workhouse in Crawley Road. Air raid shelters were built, training in use of stirrup pumps organised and a top secret evacuation plan was devised in case of German invasion. A gardener was employed

to grow vegetables and Matron given the added duty of bottling fruit.

A sum of £260 was spent on more efficient black-out curtains to conform with regulations whilst the Ministry stumped up £480 for the purchase of 20 extra beds which were to be put on stand-by should the worst happen. Fortunately there was no invasion, however Horsham did suffer its share of casualties from air raids, including one in 1943 which caused considerable damage in nearby Richmond Road, Gordon Road and Wimblehurst Road, damaging the homes of Dr.J.Westcott Dew, Dr.Morgan and Dr.Bradford as well as the newly opened nurses home at nearby Craven Lodge which had cost £3,250 to establish.

A number of German airmen shot down over Sussex were treated for injuries at the military hospital and at least one underwent emergency treatment at Horsham Hospital. Lufwaffe pilot Karl Bruning had been on a mission to bomb Liverpool in 1941 when his Heinkel aircraft was hit by the RAF and crashed at Ockley where he was arrested by the Home Guard. Whilst in the custody of Canadian Troops he was taken to Horsham Police Station and then the hospital where an operation was carried out. A ward Sister provided him with a glass of milk and some cigarettes.

Staff shortages were soon evident and the committee, under pressure from questioning at a lively 1939 annual meeting, acted to change the rules. For the first time all doctors in the district were allowed to visit their own patients in the wards, something that hitherto had been the domain of six honorary doctors. It was also agreed to draw up a list of specialist consultants who would be prepared to visit the hospital on designated days in an honorary capacity, thus beginning the practice of day clinics. The question of appointing a resident medical officer was not considered justified at that time.

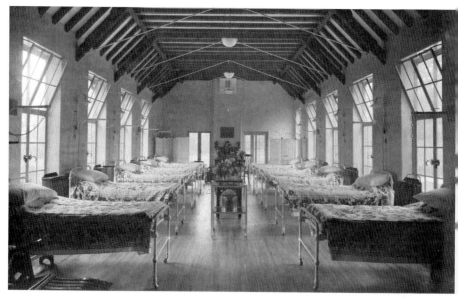

HARVEY WARD for male patients with its grand ceiling in 1923. It was named after the Reverend Douglas Harvey who inspired the building of the 1923 hospital and paid for equipping this ward.

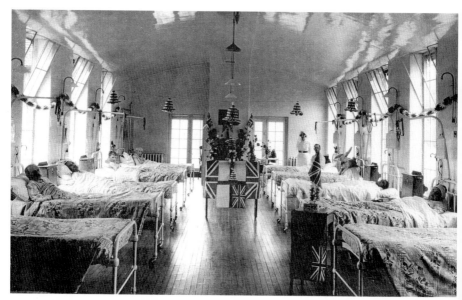

HARVEY with a new plaster ceiling erected in 1935 and decorated for a special occasion.

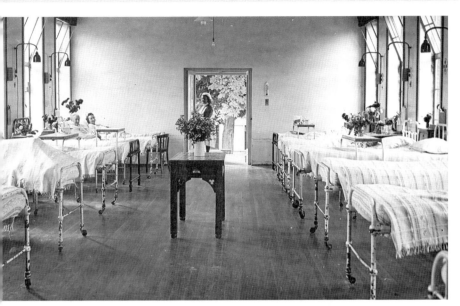

ALLCARD WARD for women was named after the Allcard family whose members devoted much time and money to the interests of the hospital.

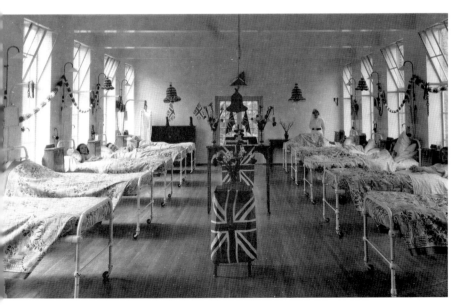

ALLCARD dressed up for a special occasion.

The interest of consultants had been aroused, it seems, by a rather unusual event in 1939 when a senior physician at Guy's Hospital Dr.Douthwaite had been taken ill whilst travelling through Horsham. He had been admitted to Horsham Hospital, was operated on by Dr.Dew and was so pleased by the care he had received for his perforated ulcer that he offered to become a regular visitor consultant and proceeded to persuade other expert colleagues to do the same.

The business of the hospital had become so hectic that by 1941 the old management committee style was superseded by a tighter House Committee which could meet more easily and more frequently. This small team must have faced great odds just keeping the hospital running, however during the period of hostilities, when bombing raids were common and aerial battles were fought in the skies above, they still managed to achieve some notable landmarks including the establishment of an Out Patients Department, a new Physiotherapy Department and the biggest achievement of them all, an entire Maternity Unit.

Their first substantial task was provision of an Out Patients area in which visiting consultants could conduct their clinics. The committee considered diverting legacies into a fund for this purpose having in 1940 received £8,000 from the will of a prominent businessman along with a succession of other smaller amounts. They also received the splendid sum of £1,463 raised at the hospital's 1943 Jubilee Garden Party held at the High School and so funds were not short, despite the austerity that war had brought to most family budgets.

Because war-time regulations did not permit, there was no question of a new building so Committee chairman Mr.Neathercoat turned to West Sussex County Council owners of the old 1892 Cottage Hospital building, part of which had been converted into a war-time First Aid Post, asking if this could be used for Out Patient work.

The county council agreed with the proviso that a charge of £20 per annum was paid for heating and lighting. Patients requiring consultations were asked to pay one shilling and six pence per visit, however the committee showed great enterprise by setting up a volunteer car pool to bring in patients from their homes, a service which evolved into the community car scheme.

Much of the routine fund raising work for the hospital would have been dashed by the war years, as many Horsham people were directly involved in the hostilities and those at home concentrated much of their spare time on the war effort. To fill the gap, a small band of worthies came together in October 1944 to establish The Horsham Hospital Supporters Association whose history was fairly short-lived but which in a period of three months raised £5,000 in order to provide a new fully equipped Physiotherapy Department. They were warmly welcomed and Frank Rowland was appointed to represent them on the main Hospital Committee.

Once more a building was needed and West Sussex County Council was persuaded to give up more rooms in the old Cottage Hospital for this purpose. The new department proved a great boon to the hospital, but it was remarkable in another way.

In 1923 the management committee had sold off this old building to the county council for £2,500 and received the benefit of that money for the building of the new hospital. Now, with the arrival of Out Patients and Physiotherapy, step by step, they were succeeding in expanding the work of the hospital in that very same building, thus returning it to medical use.

THE MATERNITY UNIT

THE question of childbirth had not been a hospital matter and the earliest rules had specifically barred women in advanced pregnancy. It was West Sussex County Council which had responsibility for providing a maternity service and for many mothers this meant a birth at home with the attendance of a midwife.

During the 1930s as Horsham Hospital began to venture into specialist areas there was serious exploration into the possibility of adding a 12 bed Maternity department and both County Council and Ministry of Health were approached on the subject. The Ministry was prepared to provide some funding, however discussions went very slowly and in 1941 the County was very much opposed to the plan, saying that it was not required.

Things changed in 1943 when Marchwood Private Maternity Home at Roffey closed down and suddenly there was a more urgent need for new facilities in Horsham. Rapid talks took place between the Horsham Hospital Committee led by Mr.Neathercoat and County Medical Officer Dr.Bradshaw during which it became obvious that there were no other alternatives and no other sites available, apart from Horsham Hospital itself.

Detailed proposals were drawn up for an 8 bed maternity block in the hospital grounds complete with labour ward, bathroom, nurses' accommodation and kitchen with direct supervisory control by the Matron who would arrange training for nurses and midwives. Administration would remain in the hands of the Hospital Committee, though financial control would be agreed in consultation with the County Council.

This was a major departure for Horsham Hospital. In the past all new ventures had been paid for through voluntary donations or the Contributory Scheme. Now they did not have to raise a penny because West Sussex County Council agreed to foot the entire bill to include the building, equipment and access road. There was one substantial donation, however, as the Hurst family once more came forward to give more of their parkland in order to provide sufficient space on which to build at the rear of the main hospital.

A special meeting of hospital subscribers approved the plan and agreed to amend the vital rule 28 which became: "Women advanced in pregnancy are inadmissible, except to the maternity block of the hospital."

Joint ventures are never easy to mount and there were many disputes between Hospital and County recorded in the minute books before the venture was finally completed and it is fair to assume that many of these focussed on bed usage. At the conclusion, the County were given priority use of ten beds and the Hospital eight.

The Unit was opened whilst the war still continued and became another valuable asset in the life of the hospital, highly regarded and much loved. There was a considerable public battle in the 1980s when health officials decided to close it down and move maternity work to Crawley Hospital, and another howl of disapproval when the service was moved even further away to East Surrey Hospital at the turn of the century.

But that is another story.

OPENED during the Second World War in 1944, the Maternity Unit was a joint venture with West Sussex County Council, then responsible for births. It served the town for 40 years and the League made numerous donations to the Unit before controversial closure.

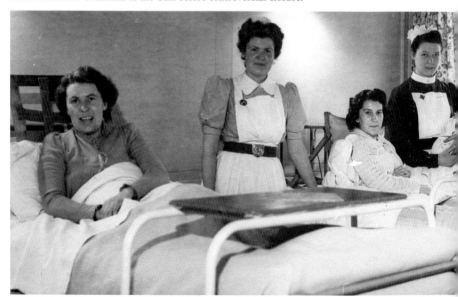

ONE of the baby wards pictured in 1949.

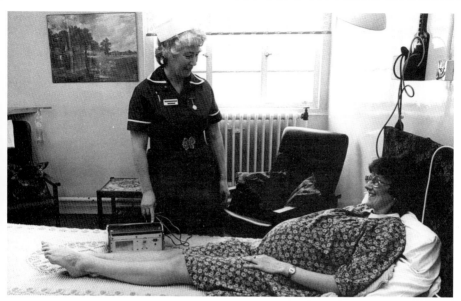

THE delivery room in 1984 with Sister Mavis Packham and Carole Sulik.
(Picture by West Sussex County Times).

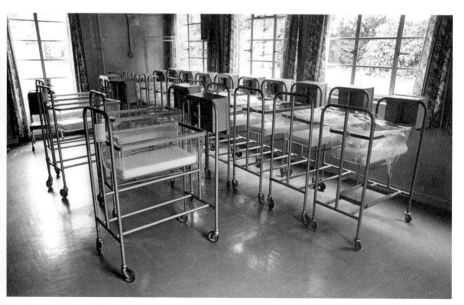

THESE empty cots pictured in 1984 heralded the end of the department.
(Picture by West Sussex County Times).

THE 'VOLUNTARY HOSPITAL' FACES EXTINCTION

EVEN before the Second World War was over many people were beginning to realise that health services had become so complex that the system would need to be radically altered, and that change would be fundamental.

Alarm bells were ringing as early as 1944 when chairman Mr.Nethercoat summed up some of the feelings over a new Government White Paper on future health services which he saw as "a serious threat to the continued existence of voluntary hospitals".

He warned the Horsham public that they would be the losers if "voluntary hospitals were manacled or slowly throttled". Freedom should be maintained, "freedom for the patients, for the doctors and the hospitals which have been built up in a pioneering spirit. We must hesitate a long time before we allow the voluntary hospitals to be swept away and the vast medical profession turned into a giant civil service," he declared.

These bold words were echoed by Dr.Bradford who spoke of his concern about the future of the hospital at the end of the war and he called for standards to be kept up and efficiency improved. Dr.De Lacy believed that the committee should seek to make a bargain with the Government and warned that if voluntary financial support was withdrawn he did not see how the hospital could carry on with a deficit of £4,000 a year.

Four years later on July 5, 1948, the National Health Service was launched and on August 8 of the same year Horsham Hospital officially became part of the NHS, winding up its life as a Voluntary Hospital.

The "town" had owned the hospital, they had built it and run it for 56 years. Now the Government was taking it away, nationalising it without any compensation. Of course, many people were dismayed, the fund raisers, the voluntary managers and the doctors who had given so much time for little reward.

Opposition to the NHS concept was powerful and sometimes bitter, particularly among doctors who visualised a socialist plot to take over the medical profession and in a national referendum a majority of BMA members voted against the new Health Act. However, Health Minister Aneurin Bevan struck a deal with the Royal College of Physicians, the consultants, offering them NHS contracts and continuance of private patients too.

But it was patients who had the final say. They could clearly see the huge benefits that would come from free health care and many thousands began registering their families with NHS doctors, dentists and opticians. The consultants were already in and the doctors had no choice but to join the party.

It really was the end of the old way; the beginning of a new era.

HEADLINE in the County Times on January 30, 1959, heralds the launch of the League.

Big Plans for the Hospital

LEAGUE OF FRIENDS SOON?

HORSHAM Hospital, which has been running an assistant nurses' training school since November 1955, held its first nurses' prize giving on Wednesday.

Friends of the Hospital: 1948-1968

The League is launched with £40 in the bank

1948-1958: A NEW WAY BEGINS UNDER THE NHS

WHAT an amazing day that must have been on July 5, 1948, when the National Health Service was launched and what mixed feelings there must have been for those who had worked for so long behind the scenes at Horsham Hospital.

The landscape had changed overnight. Now everyone was entitled to free medical treatment from doctors and hospitals alike. No more payments for ward stays. Free consultations, free treatment and free operations by specialists. No more fund raising to pay for local health services.

For all those many people who had kept the money rolling in, this was a real culture shock. The Contributory Scheme became redundant and was duly wound up having raised £50,000 in 23 years. A thousand and one fund raising events, the tea parties, the jumble sales and the annual fetes, would no longer be required to divert hard won funds towards the hospital. Gone too was the volunteer Management Committee which for 56 years had brought together so many community spirited citizens, among them the wealthy land-owners and the professionals who had so willingly devoted their expertise to the volunteer cause.

For the doctors and consultants who had given their services for free, they were to become "civil servants" paid accordingly for their work.

The management was now in the hands of a small House Committee which included the Matron, a Doctor and the Hospital Secretary who no longer owed their allegiance to a local committee but were guided by a bureaucratic Ministry of Health rule book and answerable to the "powers that be" in the Redhill Group Hospitals management committee whose remote members pontificated miles away in another county. A portent of things to come.

Having been self governing for 56 years, Horsham Hospital now faced the prospect of being part of a four tier health management structure with the policy making NHS in London at the top followed by the South West Metropolitan Regional Hospital Board responsible for strategic planning, the Redhill Group Hospitals management committee in charge of routine maintenance and their own House Committee given charge over day to day affairs.

At first many people in 1948 saw the embryo NHS as provider of everything, including all that in the past volunteers had offered without charge.

However, that Utopia was not to be. With millions of people anticipating care, a huge backlog of health problems was exposed whilst many old buildings were in desperate need of modernisation, Horsham amongst them. A cap was rapidly put in place through prescription charges designed to dampen down the free-for-all.

From its earliest times the NHS faced a dilemma of demand against resources. There never was sufficient funding at hand to meet all aspirations and it was soon realised that the new national funds conjured up by Government were not going to be sufficient at all. If patients and staff were going to enjoy all the amenities and comforts

TRAINING SCHOOL FOR NURSES

NURSES taking a break in the rest room, during the 1950s.

The hospital maintained nurse accommodation at Craven Lodge and Astonleigh at the peak of its role as a Training School for assistant nurses between 1955 and 1970.

STUDENT nurses at work in the lecture room during the 1950s under the control of a Sister Tutor.

A TEAM of nurses in smart uniforms pose for the photographer on the steps of one of the wards.

required by a hospital, then it could not be done without the significant presence of volunteers.

The NHS bureaucracy had not overlooked this and from an early stage a new organisation called The National League of Hospital Friends had been promoted in a bid to bridge the gap. It was very successful too, for 75 new groups were started in the first year and by 1959 no fewer than 600 community support groups were functioning.

Why Horsham did not form a League more speedily may seem to be a mystery, however the matter is explained because The Horsham Hospital Supporters Association, which had successfully financed the first Physiotherapy Department, continued to function and no-one at the time had any desire to replace it.

During the first few years of the NHS not a great deal of new money came the way of Horsham, though the area was rewarded by two notable official visits. The Chancellor of the Exchequer Sir Stafford Cripps came to Roffey Park Rehabilitation Centre in 1948 to open the new training centre at Beedingwood and one of the proudest moments in the history of the hospital came on Saturday, May 28, 1949 when HRH Duchess of Kent made an official day long visit to Horsham, spending a considerable time touring the hospital and meeting staff. After all the grim years of the war this really was a day for celebration during which more than 200 citizens were presented.

The Duchess was accompanied by the Duke and Duchess of Norfolk and arrived in a black Rolls Royce displaying a Royal crest. After being welcomed by Chairman Mr.John Codd, Matron Miss Horsman, and Senior Medical Officer Dr.G.S.Morgan, she enjoyed chats with staff and patients on Allcard Ward and the Maternity Unit whilst some off-duty nurses viewed her walk-about from the heights of a flat roof.

Her hectic day included a civic reception at The Ritz Cinema where she presented purses to members of the Sussex Association of Girls Clubs and Mixed Clubs, a matinee at The Court Royal Theatre, a tour of Dedisham School and tea at the YMCA.

Another substantial boost for Horsham came in 1955 when the hospital was designated as an Assistant Nurse Training School bringing an influx of young recruits and the appointment of a "Sister Tutor". The annual prize giving ceremony, at which successful candidates received badges and certificates, became a major occasion attended by NHS bigwigs and covered generously by the local press.

The Hospital Badge presented to successful nurses was designed by trainee nurse Greta Peskett in 1958 as part of a competition organised by the House Committee. It included a lighted candle and poppies recalling family donations given towards the building of the 1923 hospital in memory of First World War victims, and Greta was

THE Hospital Badge presented to newly qualified nurses and designed by trainee Greta Peskett in 1958, winner of a competition organised by the management committee. The badge includes a lighted candle and poppies recalling the hospital's links to the town's First World War memorial fund. Greta was among the first to receive the badge on completing her training.

among the first to receive it after completing her studies.

Early in the NHS era, Horsham's 1923 buildings were ear-marked for major expansion, and in due course the operating theatre was fully modernised, though it was obvious that the most urgent need was accommodation for patients attending clinics with visiting consultants. However these aspirations were overshadowed by Ministry of Health plans to spend £80,000 on a new hospital at Crawley New Town, meaning that no Government money would be available at Horsham for between five and ten years.

It is an irony that, even in the first decade of the NHS, Horsham once more resorted to local fund raising. The hospital was dealing with 40,000 Out Patient appointments a year seen by 14 visiting specialists in desperately poor accommodation and in February 1955 a public meeting at Horsham Town Hall arranged by Horsham Hospital Supporters Association announced plans to raise £15,000 for the building of an Out Patient Wing. House Committee chairman John Codd told residents that the hospital "still belonged to them" and he appealed for people to "give up two cigarettes a week" to help raise the money.

The Supporters Association had £2,000 in hand but wanted at least £5,000 to get the project underway and firmly set their sights on receiving a sum of £3,712 being held in the Horsham War Memorial Fund. In 1918 a similar pot of money had been passed to the hospital for the 1923 buildings and Association Chairman Percy Spriggs was very confident that history would be repeated. These hopes were raised when a public meeting voted in favour by 139 votes to 103 whilst Horsham Urban Council pledged to do all in its power to transfer the money. However, counsel's opinion was sought and the advice obtained made it clear that it was not legally safe to spend the money on an NHS scheme.

The issue remained a topic of much controversy with claims of "broken promises" in the local paper and an angry outburst from Mr.Spriggs on learning that the council was considering spending the money elsewhere. The outcome was devastating for the hospital. The Out Patient Wing could not be built and the bitter disappointment seems to have led to the demise of the Supporters Association itself.

By the year 1959 it had completely run out of steam and was described as a redundant organisation.

EASTER egg gift received by the children's ward in 1959 presented by staff of Horsham's Woolworths.

A ROYAL OCCASION IN 1949

NURSES were on parade, even lining the roof, for the visit of The Duchess of Kent, on May 28, 1949. The Duchess met managers, staff and patients during her tour and spent time in the Maternity Unit and Allcard Ward.

THE Duchess is accompanied by House Committee chairman Mr.John Codd and the Matron, Miss J.H. Horsman, during her tour of the hospital. The Duchess also attended a civic reception, presented gifts at The Ritz Cinema, went to a performance at the Court Royal Theatre, toured Dedisham School and had tea at the YMCA, meeting more than 200 people.

FEBRUARY 27, 1959: THE HORSHAM LEAGUE IS LAUNCHED

THERE was a new look team in charge of the hospital in 1959, Mr.L.S.Wright having taken over as Chairman of the House Committee from John Codd and Miss A.M.W.Howe assuming the role of Matron following the retirement of Miss Horsman who had given 39 years to nursing, 16 of them at Horsham. With them was a lively deputy chairman Dr.T.L.Scott and hospital secretary Miss M.B.Andrews, known to all as Molly.

It was obvious that the hospital was missing its voluntary support and these four people brought to the agenda the question of forming a League of Friends. The first discussions were held in the January when a member of the medical staff Dr.Williams introduced them all to Sir John Troutbeck, a local worthy who had shown great interest in founding such a group. Without delay a public meeting was arranged for the Health Centre in Hurst Road on February 27 to be addressed by a speaker from the National League. Appropriately enough, the building now being called the Health Centre was the old Cottage Hospital itself built in 1892.

An approved list of invitees was drawn up, mainly people considered suitable for committee work, whilst Sir John speedily organised a tour of the hospital with Matron in order to "more readily assess" what needs could be satisfied by voluntary aid. Mr.Wright put out a statement: "Our hospital needs the interest and support of all the citizens of Horsham if it is to function completely effectively." The County Times commented: "Since the hospital was taken over by the State, its relationship with the town it serves has not been anything like as close as it should be.

Part of the blame lies with the Regional Hospital Board which is just about un-publicity conscious as it could be. But the fundamental reason is no linking organisation between hospital and town."

The public meeting was a streamlined affair lasting just one hour. Admitting that his only experience of hospitals was as a patient, Sir John said he was "thoroughly convinced" that a League was needed because "while Government provides what is strictly necessary, they will not provide more." Perhaps disappointingly there were apologies for absence from nineteen people, including some doctors, however they had all expressed an interest in the League and wished it success. More pleasing they were able to count 30 members of the public in the main seats accompanied by reporters from the West Sussex County Times and West Sussex Gazette.

Guest speaker, Miss Olive Williams, secretary of the National League of Hospital Friends, outlined the many benefits to be gained from forming a League, pointing out that nearly two-thirds of hospitals in England and Wales already had one, and without further delay Sir John moved on by putting to the meeting a resolution, "That a League of Friends of Horsham Hospital be formed". This was unanimously agreed and in quick time Sir John was duly appointed the first Chairman, with Mrs.D.A.Gillespie stepping forward as Secretary and Mr.R.H.Pepler becoming the first Treasurer. The rapidity of it all was impressive.

Following a brief discussion, it was decreed that a further seven people should be appointed to make up a committee of ten. The favoured seven were: L.H.Bourne, J.W.Burch, Mrs.B.Herring, R.J.Priest, C.A.Short, Mrs.J.Smith and J.R.Stoddart. The only formality required was that everyone should become a member of the League and membership forms were distributed and signed immediately.

A draft constitution based on that already prepared by the National League was adopted with a few minor amendments and broadly speaking these laid down three major targets: 1) To foster the interest of the public in patients and staff; 2) to find funds for the purpose of providing additional comforts not obtainable through "normal" funds, and 3) to provide a link between the hospital and the community.

The meeting pressed on to appoint two noted Horsham professionals, John Ireland Eager as its legal adviser and Leslie Andrews as its auditor. There had been plans to call a further public meeting to ratify all this, however it seems that everything went so smoothly on February 27 that this step was considered unnecessary and the new committee was called to begin its work in earnest without further delay.

It was agreed that the first step was to build up a healthy membership of supporters and a list of suggestions was put forward including the circulation of leaflets to all patients past and present, leaflets in surgery waiting rooms, contact with all organisations in the town and villages, advertisements in libraries, making contact with hospital staff, local employers and simply asking each current member to recruit another.

Hospital Secretary Miss Andrews rounded off a highly successful inaugural meeting by talking about the immediate needs of the hospital, and these included a diverse range of items including a wireless system for the wards, spring interior mattresses, Dunlopillow pillows, easy chairs, television sets, waiting room chairs, flowers, vases, pictures, bed tables, entertainment at Christmas, cubicle curtains, garden furniture and telephone facilities for patients.

It was evident that the new League would have plenty of scope on which to devote future spending, when the money came in.

The historic proceedings wound up with the traditional vote of thanks delivered by House Committee Chairman Mr.Wright who wished the League every success and gave an assurance that hospital officers would offer whole-hearted co-operation in the work that lay ahead.

The starry eyed first committee received an unexpected bonus when House Committee member Percy Spriggs stood up to say that there was a small sum of money credited to the now defunct Horsham Hospital Supporters Association and, as the last Chair of that organisation, he would take steps to transfer that money to the new body.

Thus, the League of Friends of Horsham Hospital began its mission with the fairly modest, but nonetheless welcome, sum of £40 in the coffers.

1959-60: NEW RADIO SYSTEM BOUGHT FOR PATIENTS

THE first hierarchy of the League of Friends was a very distinguished body indeed. The inaugural chairman, Sir John Troutbeck GBE, KCMG, had within the first few months persuaded Her Grace the Duchess of Norfolk to become Patron and Sir Giles Loder of Leonardslee to become President.

They were supported by eighteen Vice Presidents, fifteen of whom were doctors, and it is well worth listing them: Mr.L.C.Bousfield, Dr.P.Bowen, Dr.F.C.V.Brightman, Dr. J.A.Dew, Dr.G.M.Francis, Mr.S.Hanreck, Dr.R.D.Holloway, Dr.C.T.A.James, Dr.G.S.Morgan, Dr.Alice Owen, Dr.A.N.H.Peach, Mr.M.L.H.Pearsall, Dr.E.Perkins, Dr.T.L.Scott, Dr.F.Taylor, Dr.R.White, Dr.D.O.Williams, Harry Secombe.

Tucked in there at the end was the name of the famous comedian, singer and Goon Show star Harry Secombe whom the secretary had persuaded to open the first summer fete and also join the growing list of backers.

The committee was very industrious and achieved much in a short time. Their first meeting following the launch was held on March 11, 1959, and their first fund raising event was a whist drive at Roffey, organised by Mr.Bourne, for which twenty different prizes were donated by tradesmen and which raised the "magnificent" sum of £11.8.7d. Other similar events followed, though the initial impetus was to gain members.

Sensible priority went to a publicity campaign, fixing the annual membership at "half a crown", then worth 2 shillings and 6 pence or today 12.5 pence. A membership application form explaining the aims of the League was to be delivered house-to-house across the whole of Horsham. Good backing was received from the local paper which carried regular reports whilst Horsham Library agreed to place bookmarkers containing contact details in books going out on loan.

By June 1, 1959, the League had achieved its first 100 members and with £92.19s.in the bank decided that the time was ripe to make some major decisions. First they agreed to organise a Garden Fete, arranged for Thursday, August 27, that day being early closing in the shops. Second they wanted to answer the appeal for help issued by Molly Andrews and pushed ahead with the purchase of a new stethoscope radio system for the wards for which the supplier had generously given six months interest free credit so that this could be installed as quickly as possible.

The fete in the hospital grounds was opened by Horsham Urban District Council chairman Stan Parsons who paraded on the platform with Sir John, secretary Mrs.Gillespie and Mr.Wright of the House Committee. One hour later there was another ceremony when celebrity Harry Secombe turned up via Rolls Royce to officially hand over the new wireless system, surrounded on the platform by nine proud members of the League and hospital officials. He did a jig for the audience, kissed the Matron on the cheek and cracked jokes with patients. It was a great day and as a goodwill gesture, the League sent Secombe a bottle of three star Martell brandy.

The committee had no need to worry about their lofty ambitions. Thanks to membership fees, a profit of £500 produced by the fete, a Christmas Ball which raised £60 and the organisation of a mile of pennies, the Treasurer was able to report total income in the first year of £980.

More items asked for by Miss Andrews were purchased. As well as the radio system which provided individual receivers for every patient, two television sets were purchased for the nurses' homes thus releasing another TV set for use in the children's ward, twelve spring mattresses for the wards, a telephone trolley, cubicle curtains for the maternity unit and an electric razor for use in the men's ward. Apparently patients often turned up without one. All this came to £719 and there was still £260 left in the kitty.

There is a clue as to the conditions in which the hospital was functioning when the House Committee asked the League if it would purchase a hut, "at present being used as a temporary operating theatre", so that an extension could be added to physiotherapy. They wanted to move the hut to land behind the county council owned Health Centre and needed to buy the structure for £206. The League agreed to help if the Redhill management refused.

ADVERTISEMENT announcing the League's first fete on Thursday, August 27, 1959.

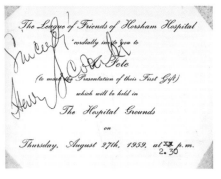

STAR guest Harry Secombe addressing the crowd before presenting a new radio system to the hospital on behalf of the Friends.

THE official fete invitation card, signed personally by Harry Secombe.

Other NHS realities emerged when John Smith of the House Committee addressed the annual meeting at Horsham Town Hall on May 4. Horsham was receiving its "full measure" of Ministry cash, he assured; modernisation and re-equipping of the operating theatre was taking place at a cost of £8,000, whilst another £15,000 was being spent on other facilities. These were the kind of sums that the ageing hospital urgently needed.

The House Committee "had very little authority, but had much influence" added Mr.Smith, and "had very limited spending powers but kept the interests of patients well to the fore." He was fully aware that much more needed to be done including a new Out Patients Department, better accommodation for nurses and a better and safer hospital forecourt.

There were many day-to-day needs that the Ministry was unable to meet and the function of the League in providing these was a most worthy one, he added. There was praise too for the nurses, of whom 21 had passed examinations since 1955.

The workload of the hospital in 1959 is nicely summed up by these patient attendance records: general wards 1,175, maternity 363, clinics 12,493, casualty 15,879, physiotherapy 15,987, orthoptics 987, X-ray 5,968.

It was soon realised that the League could provide invaluable extra services by serving tea to visitors and keeping the gardens tidy. Thanks to the goodwill of 30 volunteer ladies who came forward to keep the kettles boiling, a profit of £7 was produced and soon there were regular volunteer gardeners at work amongst the flower beds and shrubberies.

The big membership drive had resulted in 537 new members which including six corporate bodies, the Girls' Life Brigade, Holy Trinity Youth Club, Horsham Business and Professional Women's Club,

Shermanbury Women's Institute, Horsham and District Referees' Association and Gillespie and Co. Ltd.

Sir John, in his first annual report, was able to claim a "highly successful first year", though admitted that much more still remained to be done and "it may be hoped that before another year has passed, many more Horsham residents will have become members of the League".

"With so many amenities needed, it is the policy of the committee to spend its income as it is received, rather than build up reserves," he declared.

"The League could not have made the progress it has during the first year without the generous support of the public, and in particular the trades-people and the press," he noted. "As a result, the League has never paid the full market price for any goods or services rendered. Much has indeed been given free of charge, while the number of gifts supplied for the special events have been too numerous to record."

Many people had rallied round to support the League including local traders, the Horsham Urban District Council which permitted use of Horsham Town Hall at half the normal price and Horsham Festival Committee which granted free advertising in its programme.

The public was behind the League. Life at the hospital was improving. It was a very satisfactory start.

1960-61: VOTE OF THANKS FROM THE NATIONAL LEAGUE

THE brisk pace of the first twelve months was maintained as new methods of raising money were found, though the committee's ambitions to undertake a house-to-house membership appeal was not found to be practicable, probably through lack of sufficient people to undertake such a task.

Instead they concentrated on persuading the existing membership to each find one new recruit and by the end of the year a further 263 people had signed up, bringing membership up to 820.

Part of this drive involved inviting "old age pensioners" to knock on doors and for each new member signed up they would receive a ten per cent commission. The committee felt that this idea needed to be "foolproof" so that there would be "no temptations" to the old aged pensioners. The scheme did not last long and was later abandoned as many of the callers became disillusioned.

In a bold bid to bring the League to public attention they entered a float in the Carnival Procession with membership as the theme and, though it did not win a prize, this evoked considerable interest. Another garden fete was organised and despite having to cope with "very bad weather" the organisers did a creditable job in making a profit of £529 including a sum of £19 raised by members of the still functioning Home Guard who organised bingo.

The Drill Hall was taken over again for a Christmas Ball which brought in £100 though the committee were conscious that this income had been due almost entirely to the raffle and it was felt that it would be more worthwhile simply organising a Christmas Raffle in future, rather than taking on all the trappings of a Ball.

The mile of pennies venture which had begun in 1959 closed at £112 but probably the biggest success of the year was down to the volunteer ladies who had stepped up the serving of afternoon tea to visitors and by doing so had increased their profits from £7 to £56.

There was a very enterprising venture involving volunteers who were put to work manning the hospital telephone switchboard during week-ends and evenings, something that the managers much appreciated. The League was becoming more deeply involved in hospital affairs, though this particular initiative did not survive long.

Coupled with subscriptions and some surprise donations, total income came to £1,019, the bulk of which was rapidly spent on essential needs. The biggest single item was new rubber floor covering for the women's ward, where for a long time, patients had complained of excessive noise, presumably because of the solid nature of the floor surface. A sum of £360 was expended to put this right.

Patient comfort was much in mind as more spring interior mattresses were provided for adult wards along with time clocks for the radio and television amplifier. Cubicle curtains were bought for the maternity unit, "Bunnikin" china for the children's ward, and a telephone trolley whilst a sum of £75 was donated towards Christmas celebrations and £35 spent on refurbishing a donated film projector which, after overhaul, was considered to be of "great benefit to patients and staff alike".

It must have been very heartening for the League to find growing community support for their venture. The Council, the local press, the library and the Festival Committee all chipped in along with many traders. Horsham Amateur Operatic and Dramatic Society presented £20 from the profits of a production of South Pacific whilst The Horsham Town Band offered half its profits from a concert at The Capitol Theatre.

There was a note of warning in the accounts, however. Whilst the committee had spent just a little less than the £1,019 income, the balance sheet showed that they had made an overall loss on the year of £41 caused by various expenses incurred. Fortunately there had been a balance of £260 carried over from the previous year to set against this.

Sir John Troutbeck was full of praise for them all and by February 1961 he was able to say that he felt "satisfied" with the results of the second year of operations and looked forward to still further success in the future. Membership was not as large as might be hoped, he added, but what it lacked in numbers the League made up for in enthusiasm. Among his special thanks that year he singled out matron Miss Howe and hospital secretary Molly Andrews, neither of whom were members of the committee but who gave their forthright backing.

There was a nice vote of thanks to the League at the end of its second year when secretary of the National League, Olive Williams, spoke at the annual meeting on April 27, 1961, saying that she had been most impressed by what the Horsham league had accomplished to date. The joy of a League was its complete independence and its ability to give help where and when it was needed, particularly as it worked in close co-operation with the hospital authorities, she concluded.

1961-62: MEMBERSHIP FALLS – PRESSURE ON BUSY TEAM

FOR two years the League had made great strides, however it was inevitable that setbacks would arise and so they did during 1961. The high pressure of fund raising work began to take its toll whilst membership figures took a knock. Some 138 new people had been attracted to join, but there was an overall drop of 217 members, mainly because some elderly people did not renew, leaving total membership at 603.

Under the League's constitution at that

time, two members of the committee were obliged to retire completely each year without being eligible for re-election, so that meant finding regular replacements. In addition to these two departures, one committee member died and another departed with health problems, leaving a big hole in the management team. The running of the fete in August was also causing problems because so many helpers were away on holiday and a great deal of the burden was falling on secretary Mrs.Gillespie whose continuing involvement was beginning to look shaky.

Prompt action was required. It was agreed to move the next fete back to June when greater assistance would be available, thus placing fewer demands on the Secretary. Furthermore, the new post of Membership Secretary was created and given to Mrs.Widdicombe whilst Mrs.Baxter agreed to take on the tea making rota, both moves designed to "ease the burden" on the Secretary.

In spite of all this the funds continued to roll in. Lady Loder came along to open the garden fete on August 24, they were lucky with the weather and raised £576, though the Chairman was quick to point out that this success was under-pinned by generous support from town businesses along with the "untiring enthusiasm" of organisers and helpers. Entries from a balloon race had reached Italy and Switzerland.

There had been some problems at the Christmas Ball when photographers took money and orders but supplied no pictures and this event was dropped to be replaced by a very ambitious Celebrity Concert at the Capitol Theatre, organised for the League by Arthur Battle. The show featured star names of the day, Cyril Fletcher, Cy Grant and Gladys Morgan alongside a variety of local talents, whilst Matron asked nurses to volunteer as "usherettes". Grant was a big money earner at the time but agreed to cut his normal fee from £75 to just £20, the house was sold out, the event called a "rousing success" and the League pocketed £209.

The big spending project was provision of modern cots for the Maternity Unit, at a cost of £350, which were said to be much needed and would "lessen both the strain on the nursing staff and the possibility of disaster in case of fire." From this information we should deduce that the new cots were on wheels and thus easy to move.

Other large purchases included a sun-blind for the balcony of the Children's Ward and new bed curtains for Harvey Ward, though the committee very proudly announced that they had purchased something for every department that year at a total cost of £691. This spending list is worth recording here: cubicle curtains £167, sun blinds for Children's Ward £181, ward telephone £24, China and trolley for Children's Ward £25, chairs for X-ray £26, refrigerator, tables and lamps for Nurses Home £137, mattresses for maternity £19, carpet for maternity £19, Christmas celebrations £83, radios and servicing £38, clock points £4, clothes dryer for Women's Ward £5, stools for kitchen £2, leg rest for Men's Ward £5, servicing for film projector 10s.

It turned out that the donated film projector was in need of major refurbishment and the cost so high that it was not worth doing, therefore the committee was giving thought to buying a brand new one instead.

The handling of the accounts was much more circumspect during 1961. Having suffered a small loss in the previous year, the committee went for a strong profit and a consolidation of cash in the bank. The year's endeavours had brought in £1,236 of which £691 was spent leaving a very healthy £490 excess on the year and a grand balance of £709. They were still waiting to pay £350 for the cots, however this represented stability at the end of year three.

Sir John reported: "The public flock to our entertainments, the local firms and tradespeople are unfailing in their help, the local press can be relied upon to assist. There are a number of public spirited ladies who come, week by week, to serve afternoon teas for visitors and man the telephone switchboard.

"We lack only one thing – a growing membership. If every past member who has forgotten to renew his subscription would remember to do so, and if every existing member could persuade one friend to join, the numbers would begin to approach a figure appropriate to a town of Horsham's standing, and appropriate also to a Hospital that serves the district so well."

THIS film projector was purchase by the Friends in 1962 for use in the nurse training school and to provide entertainment.

Chairman Sir John Troutbeck is pictured with committee members R.J.Priest and Mrs. D.A.Gillespie, Sister Tutor S.Otway (left) and Matron Miss Lowe.

1962-63: HORSHAM GETS THE GREEN LIGHT FOR GROWTH

THE first exciting news about a major expansion came during 1962 when it was learned that Horsham Hospital had been earmarked by the Regional Hospital Board for a doubling of its size and a range of new services.

Outlining a Government white paper on the future of local hospitals, House Committee chairman Mr.L.S.Wright said that Horsham Hospital "would go on" and that plans had been drawn up for new Out Patient and Casualty departments as well as nurses accommodation in a field next to the hospital. He expected a chapel to be incorporated into the scheme and hoped that the League would undertake this part. Furnishing of a chapel would be undertaken by Horsham Council of Churches at a cost of about £1,300 whilst an anonymous benefactor had already donated £500 with promise of more to come.

Mr.Wright added his deep thanks for the work of the League which "so truly acted as a link between the hospital and the community it serves".

The House Committee began perusing the plans with some delight for the scheme involved a huge building programme which would require the employment of many new specialists and support staff. Architect designs were being drawn up and it was expected that the project would be one year in the planning.

All this meant that the League would have much to occupy its attention in years to come, however the immediate matter in hand was provision of a dedicated chapel which the vibes suggested would not be financed by the NHS and this single issue was to occupy long committee sessions. Both hospital chaplain Reverend E.D.Lewis

and Matron were strong supporters visualising a chapel being used by all denominations including visitors, patients and staff, and for the Churching of Women before they left the Maternity Unit. Services could be relayed through the wireless system to every part of the hospital and costs would be kept down if it was included in the major re-development scheme.

But the issue proved very controversial. Some felt that the NHS should pay, but the Ministry had no funds for such a scheme whilst others thought that a chapel would be the "greatest possible amenity" that the League could provide and might result in more members.

With the likely cost put at £4,000, which some members felt beyond reach, and the likelihood that a chapel would not appeal to all, the committee decided that it should seek wider opinions before proceeding. Thus a referendum was held with circular letters going out to the whole membership, setting out the arguments on both sides and asking individuals if they were for or against.

The result was that out of 450 replies, 278 declared themselves in favour and 172 against. Finally, after months of discussion and with a high number of dissenting voices the League agreed in principle to begin fund raising, launching their Chapel Fund with the £500 anonymous donation plus a further £26 collected at St.Mark's Church on Hospital Sunday.

A bid to prise some money out of the Urban District Council was made with a request that balances still held in the controversial War Memorial Fund might be diverted to a chapel, it being recalled that the 1923 hospital had been erected as a memorial to the fallen of the 1914-18 war. However, the Council responded by saying that consent from The Charity Commission for such a transfer was "extremely unlikely"

General fund raising went well and the decision to switch the fete from August to June worked successfully with The Duchess of Norfolk performing the opening ceremony alongside celebrity Gliss Anders and his toy piano. The profit was £597, boosted by a donation of £23 by Mrs.R.Priest who had organised a coffee morning, and the committee decided to book another June date for the following year.

Another Celebrity Concert was organised at The Capitol at Christmas, however Arthur Battle had been unable to book a Saturday this time and the attendance was disappointing. Thanks to the sale of raffle tickets a profit of £113 was realised, however it was decided that any future events would need to be held on a Saturday.

A total of £1,490 was spent on the hospital including bassinette cots for the maternity ward, re-surfacing of the men's ward floor with rubber tiles, widening paths and providing ramps to the wards, and the much discussed film projector was finally purchased at a cost of £173, a demonstration model obtained at much reduced price. It was felt that the projector would provide welcome entertainment for patients and would be of great service to the staff as well. Films were obtained free of charge.

The widening of the garden path outside Allcard Ward had been needed to eliminate a bottleneck to the garden whilst the construction of ramps was another safety measure to enable staff to move beds in the event of an emergency.

The committee had spent more than it received during the year, however overall the finances were in good shape with a balance of £294 in the bank and the chapel fund secured at £520. The resignation of launch secretary Mrs.Gillespie had been accepted "with the deepest of regret" on her departure from the town and she was thanked for her "indefatigable enthusiasm" which was called "an inspiration to all her colleagues".

Membership had climbed again to 668 though Sir John was not content about that. "We still need a larger membership," he declared. "When one considers the services that the hospital renders to the sick and the ready generosity of the public whenever they are asked to support a hospital occasion, it can only be a matter of surprise that more members of the public do not become members of the League."

1963-64: DISMAY AS MAJOR PLANS ARE POSTPONED

HORSHAM faced its first major NHS crisis. All the grand plans that had been debated in the previous year were now in abeyance as the re-development scheme was "indefinitely postponed". Naturally, it was due to lack of funds.

Expectations had been high and this was a real shock for the town. MP Frederick Gough wrote to the Ministry seeking an investigation into the "very serious state of affairs at Horsham Hospital". The County Times described Out Patient accommodation as "cold, rambling and hopelessly inadequate" and the position of the hospital "desperate" with only 71 beds to serve a population of 50,000. Horsham UDC attacked the "inadequate facilities" in the "strongest possible terms", whilst an Evening Argus article condemned "The Long Wait". Former council chairman Frank Holmes wrote a letter to the press visualising an "insidious plot" to let Horsham Hospital run down leading to its closure and replacement with a "glass and chrome" new hospital at Crawley.

The outspoken Dr.Scott, deputy chairman of the House Committee, told the annual meeting on May 2 that Horsham had a good hospital but that it was far too small for the increasing workload. In 12 years patient attendances had grown dramatically, and he offered three illustrations. Out Patients 5,464 to 11,104; casualty 3,820 to 15,776; physiotherapy 12,328 to 15,135.

Regional Hospital Board representatives had seen the conditions, had agreed the need for extension and draft plans had been drawn up. However, after a long time waiting for news, the House Committee had been told that the development was indefinitely postponed and, unless things changed, nothing would proceed for at least another ten years. He and his colleagues were "far from silent" and would not let the matter drop.

Dr.Scott was full of praise for the League calling it a "society of kindred spirits" and said that both Hospital and Friends needed each other. Before 1948 Horsham had a voluntary hospital built by the people for the people as a War Memorial to the Great War. The Ministry of Health had "grossly underestimated" the cost of running a National Health Service and the House Committee sometimes had difficulty in persuading them that necessities were necessary, thus the League of Friends was formed to provide amenities for patients and staff.

It was difficult to differentiate between amenities and necessities, he went on, and the House Committee was grateful for all material things. However, the League was looked upon as having a use far beyond material things. In the old days it was "our" hospital in that we all had pride in it, and a sense of belonging.

An active League of Friends could bring back to the community the feeling that the Hospital is theirs, he concluded. It was an inspirational and rousing speech but possibly in the eyes of the Redhill Management Committee it sounded positively revolutionary.

The delay was a big setback. Without the development scheme, the question of providing a chapel was considered impossible and placed in cold storage forthwith. However, the Matron came forward to suggest that both main wards, Harvey and Allcard, would benefit from provision of Day Rooms, and that these could be utilised when required as a "quiet room", perhaps a substitute for a chapel.

League members agreed that Day Rooms would be a suitable project to replace the "lost" chapel and the House Committee backed the idea, asking the Management Committee at Redhill to prepare sketch plans and costings. It was felt that these rooms would become a source of great comfort for patients and the scheme was adopted, though all the comings and goings between committees brought delays and resulted in a general reduction on spending during the year.

A total of £502 was allocated to a list of smaller items including time clocks for television sets, much needed clothes lockers for staff, new cubicle rails and curtains for X-Ray, a weighing machine for the men's ward, two fireside chairs for Craven Lodge nurses' home and a mixer attachment for the kitchen. This left a healthy excess of £646 for future needs, a useful figure if day rooms were to proceed.

Orders were also placed for the planting of conifers to help screen the hospital from a development taking place on the site of Parkfield School whilst fifteen guineas was set aside towards a nursing scholarship being arranged through the National Association of Leagues of Hospital Friends and the National Florence Nightingale Memorial Committee.

Membership had notched upwards again to 769 whilst the two flagship annual events, the Garden Fete and the Christmas Concert brought in valuable funds. Fine June weather welcomed the Duchess of Norfolk's opening address and it was the performance of the raffle which resulted in a record profit of £704. Mr.Battle and Mr.Bourne were "indefatigable" in finding a team of excellent artistes for the concert which was better attended and raised £125, though once again the major part of that came out of a raffle.

Now in its fifth full year, committee departures were becoming more regular, though the top table team remained intact for nearly a decade. Mrs.G.Baxter had become the mainstay of the tea rota, a popular and lucrative enterprise on Thursday, Saturday and Sunday afternoons, and now under the rules was required to step down from the committee. However, she agreed to continue running the rota and joined an ever increasing band of active supporters taking responsibilities for a growing range of support activities.

1964-65: DILEMMA OVER CASUALTY SERVICE PROVISION

THE new developments were on ice and the doctors had become very concerned about the state of the Casualty Department and increasing numbers of patients requiring their attention. In the light of obvious discontent, the appearance of Redhill Management Committtee chairman, Mr.Peter Evans, at the annual meeting on May 14 was anticipated with more than just the usual interest.

Although a small hospital, Horsham would not be sharing the fate of so many other small hospitals which, in the Ministry's ten year plan, were to be closed, declared Mr.Evans. The future of Horsham Hospital was safe.

He stressed that the Regional Board was fully aware of the problems at Horsham but they did not have sufficient funds to deal with them. On a positive note, a casualty officer had been appointed at Horsham for nine sessions a week with GPs covering the remainder of duties whilst the board was co-operating with the League in the provision of new Day Rooms.

Mr. Evans admitted that the NHS needed to provide more new hospitals and improve others, however he did not believe that full credit was being given to the service currently provided. He thought that the League had achieved much in its relatively short existence and its vision should be "to bring a little joy to everyone in their hospital".

The rumblings of concern continued through the year, however. The Horsham doctors believed that the creation of a new Casualty Department could be delayed no longer and had made "vehement" protests to Redhill following which plans were drawn up for a "temporary" department to be completed by Christmas 1964.

At a meeting with Colonel Legg, deputy chairman of the House Committee, Sir John discovered that even this temporary scheme had been dropped "for lack of funds" and that the consternation was such in the House Committee that they were planning to launch their own public appeal to the town. They believed that the Urban Council, Rotary Club and others would rally around, but they believed the appropriate body to launch such an appeal was the League of Friends.

The estimated cost of new Casualty and Out Patients departments, along with the

Day Rooms, was put at £75,000, clearly a massive sum which would take a long time to raise though, as an alternative, they were looking at £8,000 to merely extend the existing Casualty. Colonel Legg visualised the formation of an Appeals Committee that would be strongly supported by the town and spearheaded by the League. However, his proposals were to be swiftly dashed.

At an emotional and very difficult meeting on December 1, 1964, the League's committee unanimously agreed that the scheme was outside the function of the League and that they should not be asked to provide primary needs. The size of the appeal was well beyond their scope and the question of appealing for the larger sum of £75,000 "was not practical from any point of view".

The League said it would back any appeal launched by the Urban and Rural District councils and they did concur on one course of action, the writing of a letter to Horsham MP, Peter Hordern, asking him to press for action by the health service to ensure that Out Patient and Casualty Departments at Horsham were given higher priority.

This was quite a turning point in the hospital's history. On so many occasions since 1892 the public had been called upon to provide money for new buildings and services. Here was a crying need, but it was too vast for the League or any other local source to handle.

Of course, the League already had a major project on its hands, the provision of Day Rooms and they had pulled out all the stops to bring together a fund of £1,454 for this purpose, part due to economising and part thanks to the transfer of the former chapel fund. After consultations with the Regional Hospital Board, plans were agreed, firms invited to tender, and there were hopes of early action. Sir John was able to report that sufficient money was in hand for both rooms whilst the Garden Fete in 1965 would be based on an appeal to obtain enough to provide a third.

Fund raising had gone well again, though the idea of special Christmas events was abandoned because patronage of the Ball and the Concert was considered insufficient to make them paying propositions. Losses on the early events had been made good only thanks to raffles and it was decided simply to run a raffle instead. This project was placed in the hands of the ever dedicated Mr.Bourne whose single handed efforts raised £172 and who was duly dubbed "the League's raffle specialist".

The Garden Fete continued to thrive on the first Thursday of June, opened by Mr.C.H.Smith of Ciba Laboratories which could claim a long association with the hospital, and with a new record of £736 this strongly supported occasion had clearly become the League's flagship.

With money being set aside for the Day Rooms other spending was on the low side, with only £469 devoted to amenities, the biggest item being a sum of £97 towards Christmas festivities, though other useful items included conifer planting, a folding wheelchair, curtaining for beds to aid privacy and a food slicer for the kitchen. A generous gift had been received from donations given in lieu of floral tributes at the funeral of a prominent resident and this was spent to buy bed tables, plants and roses for the gardens.

It was also decided to make a £50 donation to St.Luke's Hospital at Guildford for the installation of "special apparatus" used in the treatment of cancer as it was felt that this would be of benefit to many patients from the Horsham area, one of the rare occasions that money was sent into another county.

Other initiatives included collection boxes in each ward and department, as well as some shops, and the promotion of a volunteer car scheme which was made available to patients, at a small charge, on occasions when the official car service was not available.

Membership campaigning was stepped up with a thousand appeal letters going out to a sample of addresses taken from the electoral register, a "membership table" was set up in the town centre in July whilst Southdown Bus Company agreed to display posters in their waiting rooms when space permitted. The result was a surge of interest with 904 signed up and the Chairman began talking about passing the 1,000 before too long. "Bearing in mind the increasing population of Horsham this should not be ambitious," declared Sir John.

1965-66: £3,217 DAY ROOMS PROJECT IS COMPLETED

SEVEN years since the launch, this was the League's best year to date. The grand target of building three Day Rooms was completed at a cost of £3,217, thanks in no small measure to another record breaking fete, whilst membership had soared beyond 1,000 for the first time.

For two years the committee had been conserving funds in order to tackle "the biggest undertaking during its short history" and there was much satisfaction when these were officially declared open on December 9. The delight was shared by Matron, who had requested them in the first instance, as well as staff and patients. The Day Rooms were a great boon and, in the absence of a chapel, occasionally served as "quiet rooms" as Matron wished.

The tricky issue of transferring the original chapel fund money had been overcome when the anonymous donor of £500 not only agreed to the change but added a further £250 to the pot. "One hopes that the anonymous donor will read this report and realise how greatly his or her generosity is appreciated," wrote Sir John.

The icing on the cake was provided by the large team of volunteers behind the Summer Fete (formerly called the Garden Fete) organised this time on an "unprecedently large scale" in order to raise the outstanding money needed to complete the Day Rooms. Hospital staff turned out in great numbers and Sir John described their efforts as "super-human", the event an immense success and the profit £1,140, smashing the previous record. Stalls brought in £620, the raffle £250 and there were donations of £300.

UMBRELLAS in action at the League's summer fete of 1966. They had set a target of raising £1,000 to spend on a new drinks machine for Out Patients and improvements to Casualty.

Opened by Mr.David Kay, at one time a patient in the hospital, the newly named Summer Fete was now considered to be one of the most successful events of the summer in Horsham. By comparison, the Christmas raffle had become a much less exciting affair though it raised a very useful £164.

Other spending was modest including two spin-dryers for the personal use of staff at the Nurses' Home, £50 towards an electric duplicator, a new trolley for casualty patients and a sum of one hundred guineas for the celebrating of Christmas. Under active consideration was provision of a tea and coffee vending machine for the Out Patients Department to meet demands there after hopes of providing a canteen could not be realised because of lack of space.

More activity on the membership front saw the League running a stall at the Round Table donkey derby in Horsham Park and another membership table campaign which resulted in a total membership of 1,004, thus achieving Sir John's aspirations of breaking the thousand barrier.

Committee members continued to come and go, two retiring compulsorily each year under the rules, and there was a succession of different secretaries but the main framework of the League remained strong with great support from the hospital itself, especially Matron and administrator Molly Andrews who devoted much time to League matters.

It was agreed and approved by the Redhill Group Management Committee that a member of the League of Friends should serve on the House Committee and the first person to take up the challenge was Mrs.B.Herring who had been a member of the committee from the very start in 1959.

The designer of the League's well produced annual report had drawn three rabbits emerging from a top hat with this slogan above it: "Combined effort and the League of Friends conjure up good things like Rabbits out of a Hat". They had certainly achieved wonders during 1965 and the tangible evidence was there in the three Day Rooms functioning at Harvey, Allcard and Children's wards.

At the annual meeting of May 12, 1965, Colonel J.F.Lomer, a member of the Redhill management, came along to bombard members with some NHS statistics which showed that costs had risen from £500 million in 1949 to £1,000 million now. The general allocation for all hospitals in the area was £2,739,705.

He praised Horsham for remaining within budget, but said that "this shoestring of administration could not be endured much longer". Conditions in Out Patients and Casualty were still "appalling". Plans for an £8,000 extension to Casualty could not be met by the NHS and he hoped that the people of Horsham would pursue the matter in some way.

Because of insufficient funds, many of the desired improvements and amenities for staff and patients could not be procured and it was here that the League of Friends, in its generosity, had proved so beneficial.

1966-67: NURSES GRATEFUL FOR HOME IMPROVEMENTS

THE League could reflect with some satisfaction on the Day Rooms project and the following twelve months were low key by comparison. Sir John in his annual report confirmed that the whole bill had been paid and the League had also responded to the demand for refreshments in the Out Patients Department by purchasing a vending machine.

It was Matron who came forward with an idea that would later blossom into the League's next major project when she suggested that the Maternity Unit needed a small extension to provide for a waiting room and consultants' examination area. This seed of an idea was, in due course, to become a fully fledged Ante Natal Clinic

With fund raising going steadily, regular donations from such as Horsham Festival and the receipt of legacies, the finances were stabilising well. Near the end of the year the treasurer was able to report £2,272 on deposit and £49 in the current account and was given approval to invest £2,000 which he promptly did by placing that sum with the Water Board at seven per cent interest.

Once more the summer fete topped the money earners with a £940 profit which included £497 from stalls, £263 from the raffle and £198 donations. The baby stall was singled out for praise after acheiving proceeds of £50. The Capitol Theatre foyer had been hired to stage the annual Christmas draw and this brought in £183. Membership figures had stabilised on 1,057.

A total of £800 was approved for spending on amenities which concentrated mainly on extras for the Maternity Unit and two nurses' homes being operated at Craven Lodge and Astonleigh. Maternity received 21 lockers, showers and a set of easy chairs which were also distributed to the general wards. The nurses' homes received a wall clock, book cases, 14 lamp shades, a sink unit, rugs and magazines plus three dressing table units and many appreciative letters were received from nurses concerning these items. A new desk and chair was also provided for the Assistant Matron's office.

Molly Andrews expressed concern because there was no-one available to answer the hospital telephone after office hours and a number of difficulties were being caused to staff and patients alike. A volunteer rota had been tried on two occasions but because the telephone was not busy all the time this enthusiasm had fallen off. Miss Andrews appealed for further help and the committee agreed to look into this area again.

By 1966 the Chairman of the Horsham House committee, Mr. J.F.Codd, was also Vice Chairman of the Redhill Group and he came along to the annual meeting on May 11 with what seemed to be very good news. An extension to Casualty could be started at last, and it would be with NHS money.

However, Horsham also badly needed a new nurses' home plus a training school and he thought that if everyone in the Horsham Urban and Rural area gave £1 each these could soon be built. The Government certainly had not enough money, he declared.

On a general note he said that the cost of building new hospitals was now around £12,000 per bed and the NHS was finding it more fruitful to build on to existing hospitals rather than providing new ones. The cost of running new hospitals was twice as much as old ones, though the actual nursing care was as efficient in the old hospitals as in the new.

He added that the town owed a particular debt of gratitude to the League of Friends and all it did for the community by serving the hospital and he wanted everyone to know how much the House Committee appreciated their work.

1967-68: SIGHTS SET ON PROVIDING ANTE NATAL CLINIC

MANY pressing needs faced the hospital, better Casualty and Out Patients departments, improved accommodation for nurses as well as all the new services promised by the expansion scheme. However, none of this was in the control of the House Committee or the League and the immediate concentration focussed on Matron's wish to see a "small extension" to the Maternity Unit.

This turned out to be a much bigger undertaking than at first envisaged as the need for a properly equipped Ante Natal Clinic was realised at a likely cost of £6,000. The committee responded to the challenge quickly, launching what they called the Maternity Wing Fund, pledging proceeds from the fete, the Christmas raffle and other activities.

Firmer estimates came out at £5,000, but that excluded furniture and equipment and Sir John called the target "no small sum for the League to find" and there was yet another year economising on smaller purchases so that the Fund could flourish. Remarkably, at the year's end they had accumulated £3,810 which included the £2,000 on deposit with the North West Sussex Water Board plus some good interest and a further £1,750 from general income.

Yet again the Summer Fete made up the bulk of this by providing £1,157, which had included the proceeds of donkey rides with real donkeys, whilst the Christmas raffle was combined with a coffee morning raising £200. Added to this were windfall donations and gifts including £500 from an anonymous elderly lady who wished to celebrate her 85th birthday by making a presentation to the hospital. A string of external events brought in very healthy sums including £324 from Horsham Lions Club's collection on Alexandra Rose Day along with other sums from coffee mornings and collections at funeral services. A growing number of donations

were coming in specifically for the clinic, including gifts from Horsham Afternoon Townswomen's Guild and the Inner Wheel section of Rotary.

Committee members were often anxious to obtain publicity in order to keep this kind of support rolling in and had agreed to issue a press release after every meeting for intended publication in the West Sussex County Times and West Sussex Gazette. To reinforce relations with the local press the County Times was invited to send a representative to actually attend meetings and the Editor agreed to arrange this.

With the building up of the Maternity Wing Fund, spending on other items was kept under very tight check with only £261 being allocated, of which £122 went to Christmas celebrations. Probably the smallest spending in a year offered by the League.

Membership slipped a little to 958 and there were the usual committee changes with the need for a new treasurer whilst the long serving Mrs.Baxter finally gave up the tea rota, though Mrs.Yarborough was willing to take over. Moves were made to bring back Mrs.Herring as a co-opted member so that she could continue to represent the League on the House Committee.

In a bid to improve communications across their wide area, the Redhill and Netherne Group of Hospitals launched a bi-monthly newsletter called The Groupvine intended to keep all those involved in local hospitals up to date with decisions and management plans. The committee welcomed this new source of information and must have been keeping an eagle eye open for some news of the long delayed plan to provide Horsham with new buildings and updated services.

A highlight of the annual meeting held on May 25, 1967, was a visit from the Deputy Group Secretary of the Redhill and Netherne Group Hospital Management Committee Mr.C.S.Thompson who found Horsham Hospital "a very friendly hospital" and believed that this was in no small way due to the co-operation between the Matron and the Hospital Secretary.

There was a great need for towns like Horsham to have a hospital to deal with patients who need not travel 20 miles for their treatment, he said. The work of Horsham Hospital had increased "amazingly" in the past 30 years using almost the same accommodation, figures showing that beds had increased from 40 to 70, numbers of patients treated grown from 590 to 1,782, operations from 360 to 902 and the attendance in the Casualty Department had moved from 186 to 14,000.

The authority had given high priority to a new Out Patients Department and nurses' accommodation but he explained that major developments were not on his shoulders but the responsibility of the Regional Hospital Board.

There was hardly a hospital in the country without a League and Horsham Hospital was very fortunate, he went on. Leagues were more than money-raising entities, they provided friendship, social contacts and relationships. It was becoming increasingly realised that communications were the real key to the hospital services. Nowadays so many professions were involved and the League of Friends could be most useful in acting as a "bridge" between the public and the hospital.

This was worthy praise for the League and a much needed pat on the back.

1968-69: TAKING STOCK AFTER FIRST TEN YEARS

THE tenth anniversary of the League was duly celebrated by completion of the Ante Natal Clinic which had taken two years of work and the raising of £4,590 by the committee and its numerous supporters. Sir John reported that it was now in full use to the satisfaction of doctors, nurses and patients.

There was a nice touch when the lady who had donated £500 to mark her 85th birthday was invited to attend the opening ceremony which she duly accepted.

The treasurer went to great lengths to provide a summary of income and expenditure since formation in 1959 and this painted a clear picture of how the League was performing. Of £18,176 raised, summer fetes had contributed £7,940, member subscriptions £2,457, legacies £1,423 and donations £1,322. Other significant sums had come from Christmas draw £870, afternoon teas £522, concerts £447 and bank interest £569. A sum of £14,887 had been spent on the hospital, the biggest chunk being £4,590 spent on the Ante Natal Clinic followed by £3,323 on Day Wards and £1,108 for television and radio sets.

The committee had survived the decade with several people still in the posts they had begun in 1959, including the Duchess of Norfolk, Sir Giles Loder, chairman Sir John Troutbeck, legal adviser John Eager and auditor Leslie Andrews. The main changes were at secretary and treasurer level, posts now held by Mr.E.R.Holmes and Mr.R.Keith Burns. The rest of the committee consisted: L.Andrews, L.Bourne, Mrs. G.W.Danton, Miss N.Gillespie, K.Parker, S.W.J.Taylor, Mrs. J.E.Yarborough.

Once more the summer fete produced £1,000, whilst the well established

SPECIAL OCCASIONS

THE League's 25th anniversary in 1984 was celebrated with a £12,500 donation to equip Horsham ambulances with resuscitation equipment. Pictured at the handover are Andrew Wales, Dr.David Skipp, the Duchess of Norfolk and Chairman Roy Budd.

MOLLY ANDREWS (left) enjoying a Christmas bazaar with Nurse Griffin.

THE Hospital combined forces with Ciba in 1951 for a float in Horsham Carnival depicting a century of development in medicine.

NURSES led by Matron used to walk to the parish church for the annual Hospital Sunday service. This picture with Miss Howe and Hospital Chaplain, Reverend E.D.Lewis, was taken on October 20, 1961.

Christmas raffle was combined again with a coffee morning and bring-and-buy sale at the Capitol Theatre raising £124. There was the usual list of small and large donations, among them a sum of £500 from a legacy.

In spite of the Ante Natal spending and a further £1,185 on various fixtures and fittings, the committee ended the year with a surplus of £1,180 and this was some measure of the success now being achieved. Current membership was 998, slightly up on the previous year, however Sir John was still of the clear opinion that it should be very much higher.

At the May 22 annual meeting guest speaker Miss D.Morris, a retired matron and member of the Redhill Management Committee, pointed to a future of larger and fewer hospitals which would bring many difficulties, especially for incapacitated patients, those needing follow-up visits and relatives who visited. She spoke of large hospitals that might become more impersonal when people were more accustomed to the personal approach in their home town.

Volunteer workers would be needed more, not only for their fund raising activities but for the more personal jobs carried out by individuals. The two aims should be to supplement the professional skills of the hospital staffs and augment the monies which were "alas too meagre".

She concluded by quoting from the Book of Proverbs: "Better is a neighbour that is near than a brother that is far off", adding "What are Leagues of Friends if they are not neighbours?"

There was one stunning shock to round off the year. The Redhill Group Management Committee had decided to wind up the House Committee at Horsham and the League took part in a meeting on November 18 to discuss the situation with group chairman, Mr.A.E.Samuels. There was press speculation about this "suppression of the House Committee" and other supposed threats to the future of the hospital whilst Sir John took the opportunity to put out a rallying call for more people to join up.

"Since the disappearance of the House Committee the League is the only direct link between the hospital and the people of Horsham and if the public cares as much about the hospital as one would gather from the press, one can surely expect them to become members of the League in their hundreds," declared a clearly angered Sir John.

Now the Hospital was being managed directly from Redhill with Matron, Secretary and Doctors merely in charge of day to day affairs.

This loss of the House Committee was a big blow to local sensibilities and sparked off a major controversy which rumbled on for weeks. Was it just a cost saving exercise, or had the committee become too big for its boots by trying to start local fund raising campaigns, by rippling the waters with scathing criticisms about lack of provision, by accusing the NHS of bad planning and lack of foresight ?

Whatever the reason, here was a turning point that would lead to many locals becoming more cautious of remote health managers who thought that they knew best about organising health affairs. There was good reason for that because the people of Horsham had a long history of running their own hospital and very successfully too.

Friends of the Hospital: 1969-1978

Battles over Casualty and Maternity departments

1969-1970: DEMISE OF THE CASUALTY DEPARTMENT

THE hospital had been dealing with 'casualties" right from the beginning and when road accident figures began to rise in the 20's and 30's a Casualty Department was being maintained by local doctors. Thanks to these town GPs a system emerged by which emergency cover was maintained 24 hours a day, 365 days a year through a rota which gave priority to the hospital over general practice.

Even after the arrival of the NHS in 1948 this routine continued and it was not until 1962 that Dr Charles Law was appointed its first casualty officer, albeit on a 9-5 basis, and the burden of the doctors was thus eased, though even then they continued night cover until 1972.

In 1969 the League had been expecting news of plans to provide a brand new Casualty Department to replace the ancient facilities that were now over-loaded, however they were in for a shock. Information came from Redhill Group Secretary Mr.G.E.Hutchinson that under new policies just emerging Horsham Casualty would be closing down, though he did his best to re-assure members at their annual meeting on May 8 that "suitable alternative facilities" would be provided to meet local needs.

There were two types of casualties, he explained, one involving serious accidents where emergency patients required ambulances and these currently did not go to Horsham, the second being minor injuries requiring GP care. Horsham was to have a smaller department which would be set up at the Health Centre building by the end of 1970. The present Casualty would not close until then, no vacuum would be created and in any event there would be no great change, he added. Misunderstandings had been created by "misleading reports in the local press."

Of course, there was big change: around the clock accident cover was over.

Future Accident and Emergency departments were to be organised on a far larger scale with centres of population of 150,000 each, thus Crawley Hospital was to

THE CASUALTY DEPARTMENT

THE Horsham Casualty Department pictured in December, 1963. It had two able beds and was handling 18,000 patients a year at that time. In 1969 its 24 hour role was ended and in 2006 a brand new Minor Injuries Unit was opened.
Picture by Evening Argus).

become the main recipient for emergencies whilst Horsham had to be content with a reduced Casualty Department, later known as Minor Injuries, which opened only during routine office hours, Mondays to Fridays, 9-5.

The shock news resulted in 24,500 Horsham people signing a petition, a deputation including the MP and heads of three councils marched off to see regional health chiefs and twelve doctors resigned in protest. Regional managers refused to receive the petition, however it was accepted later by Health Minister Richard Crossman during a visit to Forest Hospital. Anger among the GPs was high and a planned health centre in Hurst Road was abandoned by the county council because of the loss of co-operation.

All the protests came to nothing and there was much dismay in the summer of 1969 when a large board appeared outside the hospital announcing: "The Casualty Department will be closed from 5.30 each evening to 9 each morning and all day on Saturday and Sunday. Please refer to your GP or Crawley Hospital."

Sir John took the chance to say that he would like to see all the protestors joining the League, because if they did that would bring in £2,500 a year from membership fees alone. President Sir Giles Loder warned members of more "closing of departments" saying that the fight must go on. He added that the hospital owed much to the League without which it would be a "grimmer place".

The vexed annual meeting ended with the Group Secretary fending off questions, one of which related to the redundant House Committee. Not many were amused when Mr.Hutchinson expressed an opinion that this committee "was not good for

management which was the business of administrators" whilst he believed that "centralisation could be good and wise".

Later in the year on November 25 members of the all powerful South West Metropolitan Regional Health Board booked The Capitol Theatre for a public meeting to explain their revolutionary plans to deal with accidents and emergencies, an unprecedented move which illustrated the strength of feeling in the town.

The League had become well used to riding out storms and simply got on with the task of raising funds and spending it on the hospital. It had been drawn to its attention that the grounds were in a "sad state of disrepair" and the League launched into action to re-design the whole lay-out with proper landscaping, gardens and seating which could be easily accessed. The target was £3,000.

Ministry observers from a new quango called The Hospital Centre Advisory Board sent along representatives to see for themselves and after touring the grounds made recommendations which resulted in savings of £1,000. As a result, the League met with the Redhill Board and together they agreed to divert this sum to create new car parks on each side of the main entrance.

Once more, the foundation for this spending came from the Summer Fete which brought in £1,100 whilst the combined Christmas raffle and coffee morning made £200 plus a host of other donations from town organisations, including Horsham Lions Club, the Innes Memorial Fund and Horsham Bowling Club.

A sum of £912 went on a variety of small items including a new shower for Maternity, television sets, a wheelchair for use by X-Ray patients and further improvements to

Craven Lodge whilst Horsham Round Table donated a see-saw and swing for the gardens. This still left £3,595 in hand, enough to comfortably finance the gardens project.

The year witnessed the departure of keen League supporter Miss Howe after 12 years, last to hold the title of Matron during an era of powerful "Misses" which had begun in 1892. At her final meeting she warmly appreciated all the additional comforts that had been provided during her time, saying that the highlights for her had been provision of the Day Rooms and Ante Natal Clinic. Sir John called her "our guide, philosopher and friend for over ten years" who would be much missed. She then introduced her successor Mrs.F.H.Taylor who came with the title Nursing Officer in Charge, later amended to Senior Nursing Officer, though for a long time many still referred to her as Matron.

Many League members rolled up their sleeves in the January to help salvage patient records that had been damaged in a hospital fire, a bold bid was made to involve Horsham Youth Club in the work of the hospital by organising dances whilst the League's minimum subscription was raised from 2s.6d to 3s. in preparation for the advent of decimalisation in 1971, when 15 pence was levied.

Membership figures stood at 1,016 with Sir John once more arguing that more people could easily sign up, especially when one considers the "enthusiastic gathering" at The Capitol Theatre which took part in the debate over the future of Casualty.

The changing face of the NHS was becoming evident in all areas. Matron's title had gone and, with the introduction of the Salmon Report, nurses were relieved of certain non-nursing duties which they had cheerfully done before, prompting the League to set up a team of ladies who took over day to day care of flowers in the wards.

Group Secretary Hutchinson was well aware of the massive challenges faced by all when he told the League that "there was no limit to the demands that could be made on the Health Service" and "the fact that people were living longer would add to the problems". He went on: "There is, however, a limit to the available funds and running the service from the top one had to think of it as big business and had to deploy available resources to give the best possible services to patients."

The stark facts were that Redhill Group was working with a budget of £4 million a year, employed a staff of 3,500 and fed 3,200 patients every day, of which Horsham Hospital was a small part. Horsham was coming to terms with its new place in the great scheme of things.

1970-1971: SIR JOHN STANDS DOWN AFTER 12 YEARS

AFTER having played a key part in launching the League in 1959 and serving 12 years as Chairman, Sir John Troutbeck announced his decision to stand down in 1971. His energy and dedication had been an important factor in the League's success and he would be a hard act to follow.

One of his final actions was to hold talks with the Chairman of the independent Hospital Petition Committee, local journalist Jimmie Armour-Milne, who had invited the Friends to be represented on the campaign. Sir John sought further information about the ultimate objective of the petition and it was agreed that the campaigners would keep the League informed as to their actions.

Much time was spent in the search for a new Chairman and three likely sources were contacted before the retiring treasurer of Horsham Rural District Council, Reginald Fisher, agreed to take up the challenge.

Sir John was able to look back on his final year with much satisfaction having witnessed the complete landscaping of the hospital grounds and the building of new car parks for 44 vehicles at a cost of £3,152, all paid for. The general appearance of the hospital was much improved whilst future maintenance made easier too. Three public seats were installed in the area, two new and one refurbished as a memorial to the late Dr.J.Westcott Dew.

Next on the agenda was action to tackle the poor quality of flooring in Maternity where surfaces were proving difficult to keep clean and with periodic oiling could often prove slippery and dangerous. The League proposed carpeting at a cost of around £1,500, and with balances beginning to grow they were confident about finding the money.

There was a bold change to the format of the Summer Fete which hitherto had always been held on a Thursday afternoon. For the first time this was switched to a Saturday and the occasion was lifted by the attendance of newsreader Reginald Bosanquet along with a remarkable variety of 41 stalls, Horsham Borough Silver Band and Miss Martin's dancers. The day's profit was £1,075 with £235 from raffle and £75 from baby goods. The Christmas Fair at The Capitol brought in £130.

Total income for the year was £2,309 and after the League had spent £3,469 on the landscaping and a variety of smaller items, there was overspending of £1,257. However,

balances were so strong that they still had £2,337 in the bank. Matron had been concerned about the "rather drab" appearance of waiting rooms and the League quickly came up with £25 to put this right. The new flower rota was operating on a daily basis, Horsham Flower Club was thanked for decorating the hospital entrance, whilst afternoon teas continued to make steady money on four days a week though it was noted that there were insufficient volunteers to cover seven.

Guest speaker at the annual meeting on May 21, 1970, was Mrs.I.Steeds, Principal Nursing Officer of the Redhill Group, who gave members a detailed survey of the Salmon Report on nursing duties. She explained that women were being attracted into many different careers and there had been a significant drop in nurse recruitment, partly due to poor pay structures.

The Report had paved the way for a proper career structure, and had relieved trained nursing staff of extraneous duties with the aim of making best possible use of the skills available. All this would make things better for patients too, she argued.

However, Horsham lost its role as a training centre for nurses in 1970 and the rumblings over future hospital cuts and budget crises would not go away. Sir Giles Loder read out a letter received from Group Chairman, A.E.Samuels, pointing out that despite having a budget of £4 million from the NHS, the Group was finding it difficult to make ends meet and help given by the League was making a great difference to the comfort of patients and well-being of staff.

A "strong fight was needed to keep Horsham Hospital and its subsidiary services" went on Sir Giles, and the numerical strength of the League could become a vital factor.

1971-1972: PARTY FOR VOLUNTEERS IN THE GROUNDS

THE League had a distinctly new look in 1971. Reginald Fisher was in the Chair whilst the turnover of committee members continued apace with key posts of secretary and treasurer changing hands in a period of 24 months, and lots of new faces around.

The annual meeting on May 24, 1971, also took on a brand new look. The regular meeting place at the council offices was abandoned and a marquee erected in the hospital grounds to provide for both the meeting and a social evening designed to bring together many of the volunteers, £20 being allocated for refreshments.

The occasion went well, however President Sir Giles Loder could not attend because he was judging at the Chelsea Flower Show whilst Sir John and Lady Troutbeck, the expected VIP guests, also had to cancel because Sir John was unwell.

Mr. Fisher told the gathering that he had been given a difficult task following in the shoes of such a significant Chairman and it was agreed he would visit Sir John to thank him for his "magnificent work and leadership" of the League during its first 12 years.

Redhill Group Chief Nursing Officer Miss E.C.Ensing, among the guests, thought that the idea of a party was a splendid idea and she added that Horsham Hospital and its active League of Friends was the "envy of the Group". She was especially appreciative of the ladies who cared for hospital flowers and those who helped with teas in Out Patients, Maternity, Physiotherapy and X-Ray departments. She also gave Mr.Searle a pat on the back for coming up with a generator during recent power strikes.

The committee often spent many hours trying to persuade "personalities" to open the Summer Fete and regularly made approaches that failed. This time they really came up trumps when film actor John Mills and his whole family, Mary Hayley Bell, Juliet Mills and Sean Mills, agreed to come along for the annual highlight held on June 5. Autographs were on sale at five pence each, raising a total of £6.25 and the profit for the day ended up at £1,125.

The big project was the spending of £1,800 on new carpeting for the Maternity Unit, the main hospital received its first drinks vending machine following those given to Outpatients and Ante-Natal clinics whilst a bed replacement programme got underway. Minor purchases included chairs, a water heater and telephones for Maternity, as well as a small donation towards the annual staff dance.

Membership figures had fallen to 974 and Mr.Fisher took up the cause begun by Sir John by saying that this was "not encouraging" and that with a population of 50,000 Horsham could do a lot better, pledging that every effort would be made towards gaining new members.

1972-1973: 67 NEW BEDS PURCHASED FOR THE WARDS

AT last there was some good news filtering down from the NHS. Complaints had continued to come in about the cramped conditions in Out Patients and Physiotherapy departments, still housed in the 1892 building, known as The Health Centre. More than 20,000 people were going through the clinics in a year and everyone recognised that there was an urgent need for better things.

Managers announced that a bigger Out Patients Department would be provided almost immediately and that the grand plans for major hospital expansion, first mooted in 1962 and then delayed indefinitely, were back on the active agenda, currently in the design stage. These positive moves were a real boost and heralded an upsurge of activity for the League, members anticipating that they would be called upon to help provide equipment for many new services.

A whole host of initiatives and fund raising ideas were emerging driven by a combination of old hands and new blood. The long serving and dedicated Mr.Luther Bourne had taken over as secretary, the even longer serving Leslie Andrews who had been auditor from the very start, a committee member and now treasurer, was raising new money through a donations appeal. Bernard Newman had taken a big step by launching a 200 Club which raised an enormous £1,275, Bob Bruford generated £475 from the Christmas Fair and £310 from the Alexandra Rose Day collection whilst Jimmie Armour-Milne was stoking things up through publicity in the local press. As ever Molly Andrews was always in the thick of things and there was delight when she received the MBE. Always close at hand too, Matron and also Miss Sneezum who had charge of Maternity. Mrs.Yarborough had taken over the teas and was doing sterling work.

The Summer Fete opened by personality Andree Melly profited by a record £1,446, membership subscriptions were going up too with a vastly improved total of 1,320, and it was with much confidence that the main project of the year was tackled, the provision of 67 magnificent new Kings Fund beds for the wards.

This became a fully fledged community effort. The League bought 36 of them plus 32 adjustable bed tables, as well as four cots and 70 new counterpanes, at a cost of £3,153 whilst other community minded groups came forward to purchase the remainder, including 18 by Horsham Lions Club and others paid for by Christ's Hospital, Stanford and Edwards, RAFA, the Innes Memorial Fund, and Horsham Ladies Circle.

The League organised a survey of patients to find out how well the radio system was being used so that future needs could be assessed. As a result a series of transistor radios were bought by Horsham Ladies Circle. Matron also took trouble to carry out an inventory of TV sets, revealing ten in use, the annual bill for rental and repairs being picked up by the League. It was decided to obtain seven new sets including colour television for the three main wards.

There was sad news at the annual meeting on May 22, 1972, when the death of Sir John Troutbeck was marked by two minutes silence and later in the year there was a ceremony outside Harvey Ward where a tree was planted in his memory, witnessed by League members, hospital staff and representative of The Horsham Society of which Sir John had been President.

1973-1974: GREAT STRIDES MADE IN FUND RAISING

THIS was the year that "records were broken in every direction" according to the jubilant Chairman Mr.Fisher, and indeed the figures backed him up.

Total raised during the year was a new record of £5,753 and in the vanguard once again was the Summer Fete, opened by the sinister Vincent Price and enlivened by a fairground organ and steam engine provided by L.J.Searle. Actor Mr.Price spent the whole afternoon at the hospital, signing autographs, patronising stalls and even went to chat with patients on the wards. The raffle pulled in £546, the donation appeal brought £160 and with all the usual attractions provided by the stalls a record profit of £1,915 came into the Treasurer's hands.

Things were really picking up for the annual Alexandra Rose Day made £544, the Christmas Fair £620, a Carfax publicity event involving the Searle fairground organ raised another £218 and, to top it all, Mr.Newman's 200 Club enterprise, now re-named the Private Member's Draw because of legal requirements, netted £1,033

With the bank balance looking decidedly healthy, members agreed to give £2,750 towards furniture and equipment for the new Out Patients Department nearing completion along with £1,800 urgently needed to provide additional storage space for large items of equipment which nurses had been parking in the Day Rooms and corridors simply because there was nowhere else for them.

The League was also mindful of the bigger Hospital expansion plan which they learned would be very big indeed, providing 84 new beds and a range of new services which in the not too distant future would create further demands on them.

Almost every year, a remarkable array of smaller items was purchased and this was no exception. The League bought new garden furniture, a fridge for the staff, an ice-maker for treatment of patients in Physiotherapy, a "special instrument" for carrying out blood tests, speech therapy equipment, a wall clock and some small toys which staff were permitted to give to children under-going treatment.

Delegates from Horsham were sent off to Worthing in the March to take part in discussions with other hospital supporters from across West Sussex planning to launch the West Sussex Association of Leagues of Hospital Friends, a body that held its first full meeting in the May when Horsham duly became a member.

This was a preparatory move for the first major re-organisation of the NHS taking place in April, 1974, when Horsham was quite pleased to learn that it would no longer come under the control of the Redhill Board, but would be placed in the North East Sussex sector of the soon to be created West Sussex Area Health Authority, chaired by Mr.Manley Bird.

There was another big day for the hospital on November 16, 1973, when the Secretary of State for Social Services, Sir Keith Joseph, paid an official visit, inspecting wards and chatting with patients, staff, doctors and a variety of others. He did not forget the League of Friends, expressing his personal thanks to Chairman Reg Fisher for the many services given by so many willing volunteers.

Another marquee based annual meeting was enjoyed in the grounds on May 21, 1973, though it was announced that President, Sir Giles Loder, who had been with the League from almost the start, had resigned because of his Chelsea Flower Show commitments.

Mr.Fisher took over the proceedings, pointing out that membership continued to increase and currently stood at 1,350, an increase of about 35 per cent in two years. With money also flowing in, membership thriving and the prospect of a major expansion for the hospital on the way, it was a very satisfactory state of affairs.

FUND RAISING FUN

STAFF from Out Patients with their very successful tombola at the summer fete of 1984. Among them are Clover Fox, Jill Stone, Margaret Perkins, Sue Morton and Rhoda Mansbridge. (*Picture by West Sussex County Times*)

ON duty at a summer fete, Linda Mapp, Sue Morton, Margaret Perkins and Clover Fox of Out Patients.

VOLUNTEERS manning the ever popular cake table at the 2008 summer fete.

BUSY crowds at the summer fete of 2008 which raised £6,600.

1974-1975: NEW OUT PATIENTS DEPARTMENT COMPLETE

AT the annual meeting on May 20, 1974, the League remained without a President, and it was Mr.Fisher in the Chair who once more thanked the health authorities for at last providing a new Out Patients Department, to which the League had contributed nearly £3,000 worth of furniture and equipment. He also praised them for tackling the vexed question of storage and office space.

The Out Patients was so "badly needed" that it was functioning immediately, so fast in fact that it was decided not to have an official opening ceremony.

With the Duchess of Norfolk still Patron after 15 years, the committee seems to have realized that they could manage without a President and did not make a new appointment.

The Chairman was quite capable of running the annual meeting, very proudly producing a survey of the League's performance during its first 15 years which showed that out of £37,000 raised, £34,000 had been spent on hospital needs.

This summary illustrated clearly how the League's income sources were expanding and improving. Fetes and draws brought £14,628, donations of all types amounted to more than £5,000, subscriptions £4,736, Christmas events £3,270, the new Private Members Draw £2,934, Alexandra Rose Day collections £1,193 and legacies £1,423. There was even £1,614 interest received from the bank and North West Sussex Water Board where £6,500 had been invested. The sale of teas to visitors was also doing well having made £622 compared to £7 in the first year.

Spending for this period revealed that the League had given the lion's share to the Maternity Department, £6,845 in all, whilst £3,733 had gone on beds and mattresses, £3,323 on Day Rooms, £3,273 on gardens and car parks, £2,513 on TV and radio sets, £1,458 on Christmas celebrations and £1,297 on hot drinks vending machines. There were many other smaller payments for such things as flooring, curtaining, furniture, crockery, toys, trolleys, extra comforts for the nurses' home and another much appreciated telephone on wheels which could be moved around the wards.

With money being stock-piled for future projects, spending on amenities was modest. Proposals came forward for a cubicle to be added at Harvey Ward at a cost of £900 whilst smaller sums were spent on indoor games, speech therapy equipment, a safety rail in the children's ward, a fan for physiotherapy, £50 towards the landscaping of Craven Lodge grounds by boys from Collyers and the strange oddity of plastic umbrellas for medical records staff who apparently often needed to walk in the open to obtain files.

Equipment was also provided for Craven Lodge, converted to a geriatric unit when nurses moved to Astonleigh, where new toilets were urgently required and, at the request of Matron, a taxi fare was paid for a distressed lady whose husband had died at the hospital enabling her to get to London for a train to Edinburgh. A cardiac bed and hood hair dryer were also purchased with £150 from Horsham Festival.

New fund raising ideas continued to abound. A charity football match between Sun Alliance and a "Top Ten" eleven charity team raised £270 with which new blinds were supplied to wards and cubicles. The League became pioneers of recycling when Mr.Newman started a hospital waste paper scheme in the car park with promises of £16 per ten ton, and money began to roll in, sale of Christmas cards commenced and an orchestral concert was staged at Forest School. Nurses in uniform were invited to collect on the route of the annual Horsham Festival, but this offer was declined.

The summer fete raised another record £1,952, Rose Day made £618 of which half was shared with the recently established Horsham Mobile Physiotherapy Unit, waste paper made £453, Christmas bazaar £605 and another Carfax publicity day with fairground organ made £248. Membership stood at a creditable 1,511.

So prolific was the money raising that Treasurer S.W.J.Taylor reported having "great difficulty" in identifying the source of monies being paid into the bank, cash coming in without a name, and he asked urgently for a triplicate paying-in book system to help him keep track of things.

The year saw the start of the new NHS consultation body, the Crawley and Cuckfield Community Health Council, on which the League was represented by Miss Dorothy Blundy. Administrator, Mr.L.White, told League members that its main objective was to "bring hospitals and public closer together." Mr.White admitted that he did not know much about Horsham yet, however he did know that the League of Friends was doing a grand job. When questioned about the future of Horsham Casualty Department and the possibility of its re-opening at week-ends, he said he would see what could be done.

1975-1976: LEAGUE SENDS PROTEST TO GOVERNMENT

THE much discussed plans to expand Horsham Hospital, first promoted more than ten years previously, ran into trouble again. The newly named South West Thames Regional Health Authority announced "with regret" that the grand project had been suspended once more through "lack of funds".

Naturally the dismay at Horsham was considerable and Mr.Fisher, speaking at the League's 16th annual meeting, proposed that a resolution be sent to the Secretary of State expressing "grave concern", with copies going to local health managers too.

This was a rare departure, for the League did not often become embroiled in political affairs, however the decision was unanimous and on May 28, 1975, the following was despatched: "The League of Friends of Horsham Hospital have learned with disappointment and alarm of the decision not to proceed at present with the planned extension of the hospital and ask that the Secretary of State for Health and Social Security reconsider this matter with a view to allowing the proposed redevelopment to go-ahead without further delay."

Domestically, the hospital continued to do well within the very limited buildings that dated back to 1923 and the even older building of 1892 which continued to serve its many functions. There was a massive forward step when the old Cottage Hospital building, which had been in the hands of the County Council since 1922, was officially returned to the NHS following the transfer of clinics to the new Horsham Health Centre in Blackhorse Way. This marvellous and versatile building was thereafter known as The Annexe and continued to play its part with a continuous range of health services.

All fund raising records had been broken again, reported Mr.Fisher, with income of over £8,000 and a total of £10,500 spent on patients and staff. The efforts of the League were obvious throughout the hospital with new carpeting having been fitted to the whole of the ground floor, improvements to reception and completion of fitting out the new Out Patients Department. Along with numerous smaller donations, "our Hospital is now one of the most comfortable in the South East," he declared.

In 16 years they had raised £45,000 of which £40,000 had been spent at the hospital, the bulk of it on equipment and amenities.

Income was again very sound with £2,014 from the fete which included £560 from the grand draw and £734 from Rose Day, run by Mr.Bruford for five years, though the waste paper scheme had temporarily collapsed following a drop in the market. The League was stuck with ten tons of paper for a time, but managed to sell it to the council. Membership stood at a very strong 1,555.

Purchases included 18 continental quilts for the three main wards with 36 covers plus a range of curtains and rails costing in all £754, garden tools for the Geriatric Day Centre, bedside lockers, and a pair of hair clippers. Both the Chairman and Secretary, Fisher and Bourne, took on extra work loads by becoming officers of the West Sussex League of Friends at its annual meeting held at Horsham Hospital on April 21, posts they would hold for a year.

As often was the case, the Senior Nursing Officer, still known as Matron by the League, came up with new ideas and after completing an inspection of the old Out Patient Department she reported that much needed doing. The vending machine was ageing and she visualised its replacement with a tea bar in the entrance hall which could be doubled up for the sale of other League goods.

The League acted promptly. Mrs.Yarborough agreed to take on the organisation, a local builder was appointed to undertake conversion work at £101 and a further £95 allocated to equipment, including a water boiler. The job was done by December and 15 lady volunteers were ready primed to open the hospital's first Tea Bar on January 5, 1976.

The year ended, however, with ominous "rumours". Nursing officer Miss P.M. Sneezum had heard talk of impending closure of the Maternity Unit which was very worrying to all connected with it, she told the League. It was a great asset to the town and

district and once closed it would never re-open again, she warned.

The committee's long serving Leslie Andrews thought that the League should express "grave concern" to the Health Authority and the Chairman undertook to see that this was done.

1976-1977: DEVELOPMENT SCHEME BACK ON AGAIN

THERE was no further development on the threatened Maternity Unit, instead the League received great news that their protest to the Minister seemed to have worked wonders: the major redevelopment plan was back on the agenda, though would take some time in the planning and building.

The Chairman could report "another record year" at the annual meeting on May 24, 1976. Income had been the highest ever at £12,554 whilst administration costs had been kept down to £233, thanks to the degree of volunteer support from so many different people at many different levels.

Work was expected to begin on the extensions during the current financial year and "although there may be few signs of progress on the site at present" Mr.Fisher had been informed that it was all systems go and that the League would "undoubtedly" be called upon to provide many new amenities, additional to the those proposed by the NHS.

"Your committee has, therefore, thought it necessary to conserve part of the League's funds for this purpose," he added.

New saving began, but plenty was done for the hospital. Thirty-three fire resistant lockers were purchased for Harvey, Allcard and Children's wards at a cost of £1,494. The usual long list of smaller items were funded and League members entered into commitments to double the size of the Day Rooms at a cost of £6,374, put aside £500 for furniture and £130 for more garden furniture bringing the latest spending tally to £11,000.

Special tributes were paid to porter Mick Cope who retired after 39 years service, described as a great friend and worker for the League, always ready to provide a helping hand. His role was regarded with such admiration that it was agreed to re-name the children's ward which thereafter became Cope Ward. Farewell was also said to retiring solicitor Mr. John Eager who had given 21 years to the League.

Jean Marsh, known as Rose in the TV drama Upstairs and Downstairs, proved to be a big attraction at the Summer Fete on May 29 along with Mr.Searle's Gavioli fairground organ and the proceeds hit a new high of £2,497. Thanks for finding the celebrity were due to Mr.Laurence Evans of Chesworth House, a regular supporter who had been helping out with fete openers for several years.

Rose Day was now being run by Round Table and made £502, from which a donation was made to the newly formed Friends of Roffey Park and St.Christopher's. Other income included £175 from the town collection, £202 from Christmas cards, £620 from the Christmas bazaar run by new member Roy Budd, £900 from the Private Members Draw and a surprise sum of £1,893 from the revived waste paper project. It seemed that there was great money to be had simply by inviting people to drop discarded newspapers and magazines into a container in the hospital car park.

The new Tea Bar was doing well in its first year and, although it was not intended to make profit, its charges were so reasonable that a surplus of £290 had been recorded.

To cope with all the extra activity, the League's constitution was amended to allow for a committee of twelve rather than ten, whilst members retiring after three year stints were now eligible for re-election. This proved a boon and prevented the premature loss of hard working volunteers.

Chairman Fisher compiled a long report in which he paid ample tribute to the hordes of volunteers now helping the hospital adding that the League had "come a long way" since its foundation in 1959, praising the founders for their initiative and the community for its excellent support. The League's growth could be illustrated by the 1959 income of £980 compared to the current figure of £12,554.

"In the coming years there will be increasing demands for the League's services and inflation as well as the extension of the Hospital will add to the cost of providing amenities," warned Mr.Fisher, urging everyone to continue the "magnificent support" so that Horsham could have a hospital "of which any town could justly be proud".

1977-1978: LEAGUE TO PAY FOR NEW COURTYARDS

MUCH to the delight of all concerned, builders began work on the long delayed hospital extension on acres of land to the side of the Hurst Road premises, a scheme that would more than double the size of the hospital and bring modern facilities and new services.

The plans revolved around the growing elderly population with 84 beds for geriatric patients, clinics, rehabilitation centre, physiotherapy, hydrotherapy, occupational therapy, speech therapy and a host of support functions including pharmacy. The most exciting aspect was the "modern" design, everything provided on one level with patients given freedom of movement into protected courtyards and a "village street" area where patients could meet, talk, shop and enjoy a cafeteria.

The philosophy was to give patients the chance to live as full a life as possible, to increase self-respect and independence and to provide many of them with a chance to resume their lives at home after periods of infirmity.

The League agreed a policy to spend money where otherwise the NHS could not afford to pay and immediately committed a sum of £10,500 to cover the landscaping of three inner courtyards, a gesture which one of the medical consultants called "a major contribution toward the running of the hospital".

Records were still being set by the fund raisers. Total income was £13,420 with administration costs of only £354, membership soared to 1,620 and there was still plenty of energy being devoted to existing departments. Day Rooms at Harvey and Allcard wards were doubled in size and given new carpets, curtains and furniture at a cost of £7,545, and the League then ploughed £2,237 into urgently needed improvements to Physiotherapy still functioning in the 1892 building, now referred to as The Annexe.

Even after all this spending, former auditor now treasurer Leslie Andrews, who had been with the committee since its foundation, could report to the May 23 annual meeting that the League had gathered together a surplus of £18,000

Another record came from the fete which chalked up £2,737 with actor Tony Britton the star attraction. Rose Day made £677 from which a donation was made to the physiotherapy department at Forest Hospital, Christmas bazaar £766, Christmas cards £259, a street collection £263, the Private Members Draw £917 and waste paper brought in a staggering £2,935 during a year when prices at the mills were higher than usual.

There was a long list of donations and legacies totalling £2,179 derived from pubs, scouts, concerts, social clubs, whist drives, dances and generous individuals all prepared to give thought to their local hospital.

With hospital managements and policies changing on a regular basis, the League's importance as a source of continuity in hospital life became more apparent and part of the routine was to mark the departure of long serving staff or special retirements. Members said farewell to Dr.Ronnie White, a town GP for 30 years, to Sister Pritchett of Maternity, Sister Rist of Casualty, and receptionist Ethel Mason, all of whom had given dedicated service over long periods.

"We have every right to feel proud of our achievements," noted Mr.Fisher, "but they would not have been possible without the marvellous support which we continue to receive from the local community". His theme was now a familiar one, but it was a fact: the people of Horsham continued to rally round their precious hospital.

1978-1979: MATERNITY UNIT CLOSURE PLAN OPPOSED

THE rumours first detected by Miss Pat Sneezum had proved correct. The health authorities wanted to close the much prized Horsham Maternity Unit and centralise this service at Crawley Hospital.

The news was received with dismay by League members. Although the Unit had been financed by West Sussex County Council back in 1944, volunteer fund raisers had poured money into this department for nearly 35 years and it was considered to be at the heart of the hospital's services.

The League made it quite clear that it was "strongly opposed" to the closure, part of a new three year plan drawn up by the West Sussex Health Authority, and sent off a strongly phrased letter to that effect. The unit had given excellent service to the area over many years and the League informed the authority that "any proposal to close it would be contrary to the wishes of the vast majority of local inhabitants."

Chairman Fisher's prediction was right. Hundreds of people were soon marching through the streets of Horsham with banners in a huge campaign to prevent closure.

League representatives were in an unusually militant mood over other worrying implications. They opposed transfer of maternity beds to psycho-geriatric use, they objected strongly to ante-natal moving to the new town centre based Horsham Health Centre, they argued for the retention of general and acute beds and even went as far as to protest about the allocation of 15 beds in the new development intended for psycho-geriatric use. On top of all that they called for assurances about the opening hours for Casualty.

It was the biggest broadside ever fired by the League and the Chairman was given full powers to stress the situation, told to emphasise the rapid growth of Horsham and the increasing number of young married couples in the town. The League had been drawn into another political battle on a par with the downgrading of Casualty.

On the positive side, hospital building work was now "making very good progress" and expected to be finished at the end of the year, though with many months of equipping and commissioning. As well as paying for three courtyards, the League had agreed to buy two further mobile telephone units and was looking at various other "extras" including a Hospital Shop. "We do not intend to supply those items which can, and should, be provided by the State," stressed Mr.Fisher.

Financially, the League was looking more stable than ever. Another record sum of £14,065 was raised, and the general fund stood at £30,085. However the committee was deliberately building up funds for the future and had begun making serious investments which included £16,569 in the National Savings Bank and £12,031 with Horsham Building Society, both of which were generating healthy income.

Significant sums came in from regular sources including a handsome £3,164 via the fete opened by TV star Richard Briers who signed 520 autographs at five pence each, attracting an estimated 3,000 people. Waste paper made £1,771, donations and legacies £1,635, Private Members Draw £1,037, Xmas bazaar £910, Rose Day £629 of which £157 was given to Dedisham, Memorial donations £542, Street collection £355 and Christmas cards £304.

Routine spending on smaller items and regular commitments such as TV sets, telephones, vending machines and Christmas grants came to nearly £2,000, including provision of a fish tank on Cope Ward and a piano for Craven Lodge.

Key retirements included Senior Nursing Officer Mrs.Taylor "a great supporter of the League", temporarily replaced by Sister Joy Lampard, and secretary Luther Bourne, another stalwart who had been a founder committee member and "played a large part in the success of the League" to be succeeded by Mrs.Joan Yarborough, another who had undertaken many duties including the tea bar project.

The 20th year celebrations were led by the Chairman who highlighted increased income from £580 in the first year to £14,065 in the 20th, "a creditable performance even allowing for inflation" he added.

During 20 years since 1959, the League had raised £95,784, of which £58,221 was generated in the past five, £75,000 had been spent on amenities and comforts, whilst there was still £30,085 in the bank. There was, however, no time for complacency as the League was getting into gear to supply many items which would undoubtedly be required in the greatly enlarged hospital.

THE PHYSIOTHERAPY DEPARTMENT

THE first Physiotherapy Department set up in 1945 in the 1892 building thanks to £5,000 raised by the Horsham Hospital Supporters Association which wound up in 1959.

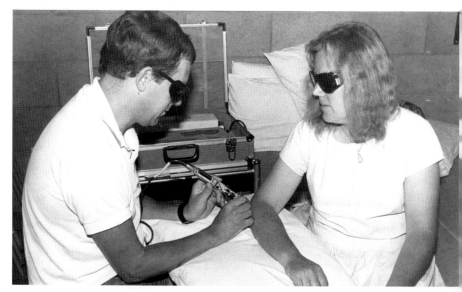

LASER treatment being given by John Jordan in the fully equipped Physiotherapy Department established in the 1981 extensions.

THE modern gymnasium and fitness equipment.

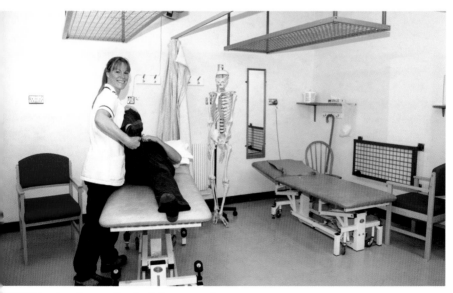

SMART treatment rooms for physiotherapy work.

Friends of the Hospital: 1979-1988

New services arrive with major expansion

1979-1980: NEW TEA BAR AND SHOP LAUNCHED

THIS was a very big year for the League. The inspirational Reg Fisher stood down as Chairman, Molly Andrews announced her retirement as Hospital Administrator, the Maternity Unit storm raged and building of the "new" hospital advanced steadily.

Bank manager Roy Budd became Chairman and the committee line-up in the June looked like this: Chairman R.J.Budd, Vice-Chairman B.J.Newman, Secretary Mrs.J.Yarborough, Treasurer L.H.Andrews, Auditor R.E.Greatorex, Membership Secretary W.G.Counsell, L.H.Bourne, R.L.Fisher, F.H.Hughes, F.Tilling, Mrs.J.Huke, Mrs.G.Tilling.

Of these, Leslie Andrews and Luther Bourne were survivors of the first 1959 committee now entering their third decade of service. Also in regular attendance at League meetings ever since the start, Miss Andrews, a co-founder of the League and devotee ever since.

West Sussex Health Authority came back with a quick riposte to the League's stinging protests. Views on the Maternity Unit "were understood and appreciated" however improvements in the fields of mental health and care of the elderly could only be attained by the "rationalisation of other services". The balance between acute and geriatric beds would be "carefully observed", whilst they had to act to end the district's shortage of psycho-geriatric beds.

With regard to the future of medical and surgical cases, the news was not promising either. With Crawley being extended and Cuckfield being replaced, it would be "impossible to promise Horsham any extended acute facilities before the end of the century" came the response.

The writing was on the wall. Front line services were going to disappear from Horsham completely as Crawley Hospital and the planned Princess Royal at Haywards Heath would assume responsibility.

On a brighter note, the League pressed on with its £10,500 contribution towards landscaping the new courtyards and began looking forward to completion of all new buildings in early 1980. In one of her final reports to the League, Molly Andrews asked if volunteers would take on the responsibility of running a cafeteria/tea bar, a shop or a patients club which were to become part of the 'new look' hospital.

Following lengthy discussions, League members made a firm commitment to run the cafeteria which they assumed would replace the tea bar in The Annexe. If sufficient volunteers came forward, and one agreed to act as a manager, they were also minded to take on the shop, though they did not object should the WRVS wish to step in. There was a vote against any League involvement in running a bar or social club for patients.

There was nearly a year to prepare for these big moves. New buildings were due to be handed over by January, the kitchens were due to be running by May and a gradual occupation of the wards was expected to start in August 1980.

Patron Lavinia Duchess of Norfolk was taken on a hospital tour on July 10 to see for herself some of the League's main achievements. She was so impressed that she invited the whole of the committee with their partners and up to 80 members of staff to a cocktail party held at Arundel Park in the following September for which several coaches were booked and a "splendid evening" enjoyed by all.

There was another landmark when four members of the League attended the 30th anniversary gathering of the National Association of Leagues of Friends held at Goring where they were presented with a certificate recognising Horsham's 20 years of achievement, this duly framed and hung in the hospital. At the same time, a bid was being made to launch a League of Young Friends by calling on the support of sixth form students. Unfortunately it did not progress far.

The fete on May 26 was restricted by very wet weather however still managed to raise £3,291 with £1,096 from the draw and £379 from the donation appeal. Waste paper came up trumps again with £1,526, member subscriptions brought in £1,799, Christmas bazaar £1,147, Rose Day made £528, and street collection £303. The tea bar was making steady monthly profits in the region of £45 and volunteers took on a new venture running a coffee stand at Leonardslee Gardens at the invitation of Sir Giles, proceeds going to the League.

With the extended hospital now imminent, the committee agreed another wave of spending to spruce up the new buildings. They committed £3,428 to provide garden furniture consisting of 60 chairs, ten tables, seven sets of seats and nine umbrellas, whilst a figure of £1,300 was agreed for the purchase of 142 trees to be planted around the perimeter. As a bonus they voted to put aside £7,000 for extra toilets at Allcard Ward in what was now being regarded as the "old" hospital, whilst they paid £700 to send the Midwifery Sister on a special course called Preparation for Parenthood as no NHS funds were available for this.

This decision had its irony for it was at the same time that the bosses were planning to take Maternity away from Horsham.

There was also a "very long list" of other smaller items including TV sets, games, vases, trowels, mirrors, text books, projectors, and a whole host of items which, once more, the NHS could not cover. No year went by without the League happily forking out for similar lists of miscellany.

1980-1981: HOSPITAL EXTENSION BEGINS TO TAKE SHAPE

THE £2.5 million New Wing was finally built, the biggest sum invested by the NHS in Horsham so far, however there was insufficient money for all the many different services to begin at the same time, so a period of "phased" operation began.

The kitchens got going, serving the whole hospital, the Cafeteria began work and Physiotheraphy moved over, enabling The Annexe to close down for major refurbishments. Because of this the League lost its main store-room and the search began for a new one.

November 1, 1980, was declared opening day but only one of the three wards was working with just 28 beds out of the planned 84. Consultant Geriatrician Dr Tony Martin spoke to the League about a shortfall of equipment on this ward, including trolleys and monitors, asking for £4,500 to bridge the gap. Until this time the League had avoided buying large pieces of medical hardware, believing that this was the duty of the NHS but, with national funds sorely stretched, it became clear that policy needed to change radically. During 1980 the League bought seven pieces of medical equipment costing £16,658, including an ambulatory monitoring system at £7,670 and a £2,500 cardiac monitor for use in the theatre.

They fulfilled the promise to landscape courtyards at an increased cost of £11,781 which Leslie Andrews called money well spent because of the "therapeutic" value of flowers and shrubs to patients. The usual array of smaller items included clocks for all new rooms, GPO trolley telephones, hoists, games and smaller pieces of equipment. A request to provide decorative prints for the foyer planned by an NHS "interior designer" was not greeted with the same enthusiasm.

There was good news from West Sussex HA to say that a decision on the Maternity Unit had been "deferred" and Chairman Budd wrote them a letter expressing the League's "pleasure" at this, though adding "displeasure" over the disappointingly slow activation of the New Wing.

New hospital administrator Tony Mills and new Senior Nursing Officer Miss R.Roberts were welcomed by the League and there was a fond farewell for Molly Andrews who had devoted more than 30 years to backing voluntary work. A fitting tribute was paid when the main thoroughfare of the New Wing was named Molly Andrews Way, a plaque paid for by the League, whilst Molly was featured in the local paper in a photograph with her namesake, film star Anthony Andrews under the heading "Andrews meets Andrews".

A former salesman on the County Times, Mr.Andrews had returned to the town to open the summer fete which proved another success by raising £3,300, including £1,202 from the draw, £805 from donations and £1,907 from stalls.

Membership hit a new peak of 1,922 in spite of subs going up from 15p to 25p, the first increase in 21 years, and income continued to flourish with £2,370 from waste paper, £1,163 from Christmas bazaar, £950 Private Members draw, £399 street collection, £150 from Christmas cards and bank interest of £590. New funds were also coming in from the sale of Frank Holmes book on hospital history, the proceeds of which were donated to the League.

The League continued to spend liberally on the hospital but had also accumulated very healthy surpluses which were placed into money making investment accounts, so that they could call on a general fund of £45,000.

1981-1982: BARONESS DECLARES NEW WING OPEN

THE official opening of the New Wing took place on March 25, 1981, when a plaque was unveiled by Baroness Robson of Kiddington, chairman of the South West Thames Regional Health Authority, though the occasion was not particularly auspicious.

Half of the buildings remained un-used while the League was a little miffed because their President, the Duchess of Norfolk, had not been invited. Health managers later agreed to take her on a tour once all wards were open.

The new premises hosted the League's annual meeting for the first time on May 18 when Roy Budd spoke of "a very successful and exciting year". He expressed disappointment that the New Wing was not working fully but had been assured that all three wards, Oak, Ash and Beech, would be operational soon.

The newly appointed Head of Geriatrics and Medicine for Horsham and Crawley, Dr Martin, praised the League for its "tremendous generosity" in the buying of new equipment and announced that the new Horsham unit was the first of its type in the whole of the United Kingdom, and a "first" for Horsham.

There were some awkward questions from the floor regards the League's accumulated funds by a speaker who called for urgent refurbishment of the nurses' home. The Chairman defended committee policy by stressing that money was being held until the future direction of the hospital was clear, particularly with regard to the fate of Maternity, the use of The Annexe, the opening of the New Wing and a commitment by the League to open a shop.

Health watchdog The Community Health Council called a public meeting on the Maternity issue in March when further opposition was voiced. Figures showed that use of the Unit had declined and both the League and Maternity consultant Mr.Booth supported proposals to reduce the number of beds to eleven as a means of saving it. The struggle would continue for a few more years yet.

News came through that the 1892 built Annexe would be refurbished and returned to hospital use quickly with a sum of £3,900 received from the District Lottery being used to provide the old building with a proper lift. Its latest lease of life was a Psycho Geriatric Day Centre with the re-opening of wards that had once played a part nearly a century previously.

Star of Yes Minister Paul Eddington braved bad weather on June 9 to open the summer fete which brought in another £3,250 and in August the League set up a sub committee to plan for the hospital's first shop. The WRVS had been interested but thought it better if the League did the job and it was finally agreed to launch the project on January 4, 1982, opening between 2-5pm from Monday to Friday, with an initial stock fund of £750. Signs were ordered and insurance implications studied.

Significant sums came in from Christmas bazaar £1,241 and waste paper £868 whilst the new Tea Bar, rather than the planned 'Cafeteria', was doing a steadily increasing trade bringing around £75 a month. Membership slipped slightly to 1,847 but the year ended with £47,000 in hand, the main spending being £5,000 on blinds for Harvey and Allcard wards, £800 for furniture in the AnteNatal clinic, colour TV sets and a vending machine at £795. Requests for a de-luxe vending machine to provide meals for night staff was turned down because of the estimated cost of £4,500.

Discussions about providing a new hospital radio system to serve all 140 beds at a cost of £1,876 received active consideration but no decision was reached.

THE 1981 EXPANSION

A £2.5 million expansion of the hospital was completed with an official ceremony on March 25, 1981. The League landscaped new garden courtyards and, for the first time, purchased expensive medical equipment.

SMART new wards in the new wing were named Oak, Ash and Beech.

THE hydrotherapy pool.

WORKSHOPS in the occupational therapy section.

1982-1983: SOME ASSURANCES ON HOSPITAL'S FUTURE

THE commissioning of the New Wing was fraught, however its arrival would ultimately be a triumph for Horsham. Whilst other small hospitals were closing, Horsham Hospital was expanding, taking on new services, and the future was more assured, even though the nature of work was different.

As well as the new Oak, Ash and Beech wards, there were brand new buildings for a range of special services including occupational therapy, physiotherapy, speech therapy, hydrotherapy and a day hospital where the elderly could receive help and training to enable them to continue normal lives after serious illnesses, named the John Ingham Unit, after the architect who had designed the revolutionary single storey complex. The local press dubbed it "a five star hospital".

There continued to be regular scares about the future as health policies changed, new managers came in and new authorities took command and it was to relieve one such alarm in January 1982 that Peter Catchpole, district administrator for the Mid Downs Health Authority, attended a League committee to give his assurances.

The wave of public concern centred on growing numbers of Horsham patients being required to travel to Crawley for treatment but Mr.Catchpole said he expected Horsham to have more consultants, new clinics and more minor operations, with dental surgery soon to begin. He admitted that ear, nose and throat work could be moving to Crawley following the retirement of Mr.Bates, who had operated a high level of service, however he pledged that the League would be fully consulted before any changes happened.

The New Wing was now fully operational with the last department, Occupational Therapy, having moved in along with a £359 hydraulic table provided by the League whilst the long awaited Hospital Shop was up and running, making a profit of £68 in the first two months.

League policy was shifting significantly. More money was being spent on hospital equipment, previously the domain of the NHS, and the main source of income was no longer the fete but interest received from bank deposits and investments, such was the large sum in hand. Members also began making gifts outside the hospital, including aid for the setting up a 20 bed unit at Forest Hospital, and had sought to change the League's constitution, however The Charity Commission declared such payments in order.

More income was being received via wills including a significant sum of £26,000 from a former patient part of which was placed into gilt edged investments, £2,749 was earned from the fete, £1,219 from Christmas events, £570 Private Members Draw, £280 street collection, and by the end of the year there was a record pot of £87,210 in hand.

This was a remarkable situation because the League continued to spend too. In April the committee approved nine projects which included auto bathing lifts for Oak and Beech wards costing £1,533, a huge list of incidentals for Occupational Therapy, patient alarms, garden furniture for Willow Day hospital and even a bird cage and stand costing £28 which would be "good for patients".

In June there were requests for a daunting array of 28 items, most of which were agreed, including a £7,250 operating table, £1,600 heart and blood pressure monitor, £856 portable ultra-sound machine, £556 speech therapy kit, £550 spirometer for the chest clinic, £645 ECG machine for Out Patients and a £655 ultrasonic unit for Physiotherapy. Chairman Budd wrote to health managers asking for assurance about the future of the Operating Theatre before big orders were placed and received an optimistic response saying that development of minor surgery was being encouraged.

There seemed no end to the small bills that the League approved. It cost them £611 to have 21 telephone points connected in the New Wing so that Trolley Phones could be utilised. They also gave £30 for an Accident and Emergency manual for the casualty sister, and they granted the marvellous sum of 60 pence per month for the feeding of the hospital's goldfish. The New Wing was keeping the committee very busy indeed.

The Duchess of Norfolk was able to make her private visit on April 14 which she enjoyed in the company of Roy Budd and Andrew Wales, however afterwards the Chairman expressed his "horror" at the state of the new gardens for which the League had given more than £11,000. Clearly they were not being properly cared for, he said, and felt badly let down by the health authority who had asked for the gardens in the first place. In the absence of any other solution it was agreed to seek new volunteers to tidy them up and provide care on a regular basis.

The year ended on a happier note when a framed notice was put up in the main foyer of the New Wing displaying a complete list of all the League's spending in its first 23 years. The sum came to more than £100,000.

1983-1984: CELEBRATIONS FOR 25TH ANNIVERSARY

IN its landmark 25th year the League's treasurer ascertained that a grand sum of £140,367 had been spent for the benefit of the hospital since 1959. The biggest amount had been spent on diagnostic and medical equipment, £15,582 in all, whilst £11,910 went on landscaping, courtyards and gardens for the new extension, £10,327 on three Day Rooms and £10,035 on eye equipment. Other sums were spread all around the hospital, not forgetting £9,899 on television sets.

During this special year, volunteers amassed another £26,457 and spent just a bit more, £27,485, of which more than £20,000 was allocated to valuable medical equipment.

Around £9,000 of this went to improve conditions in Mr.Spolton's Eye Clinic including a precious early glaucoma detection kit, the Operating Theatre received a £1,720 heart monitor and Ante Natal Clinic got a £6,300 ultrasound scanner. These were significant purchases in the anniversary year and all helped to save many patient journeys to Crawley, Cuckfield and Redhill.

Chairman Budd was full of praise for the pioneers who had launched the League in 1959 in order to provide amenities that were outside the scope of NHS funding. "The picture has never changed," he reported, "and probably the situation is now far more serious than it was some 25 years ago."

He picked out Sir John Troutbeck for special mention, and also Luther Bourne who had organised the first fund raiser and had served prominently on the committee for almost the whole 25 years, only now retiring because of ill-health. He also recalled Dr.Scott's words of 1963 when he called the volunteers "a society of kindred spirits", adding, "We are still in 1984 working together in many ways for our hospital".

Support continued for the retention of the Maternity Unit whilst the League was seeking an early meeting with Mid Downs Chairman Martyn Long to persuade him that there was a good case for making greater use of the now ageing Operating Theatre.

The Hospital Shop made a useful start, however the committee realised early on that it was not in the best location and a plan was devised to have new premises built by the works department much closer to the thriving Tea Bar, at a cost of £3,440. This work was completed by the end of the year whilst the old shop was converted into a much needed store-room and office for the League.

The summer fete of 1983 was hit by heavy rain and the whole event moved inside, however DJ David Hamilton, the son of a Rudgwick farming family, proved a big attraction, signing autographs in the packed corridors and paying a visit to the Maternity Unit where he chatted with new mums. The day realised £2,637 whilst other money flowed from donations £3,172, subscriptions £2,857, Christmas events £2,185, Waste Paper £2,143, Private Members Draw £1,170 and bank interest of £10,570. The tea bar was now thriving with a profit of £933 and the shop not far behind on £590. Assets at hand in the February of 1984 stood at a very substantial £91,662.

There was sad news in August when the death of Reg Fisher was announced and the committee held a minute's silence for their former Chairman whilst a project was put in hand to purchase new equipment for the Maternity Unit in the form of a memorial.

Many hours were spent deliberating how best to mark the 25th anniversary. The previous Chapel scheme was revived but considered very costly. There was a desire to fully modernise Allcard Ward but this cost was put at £60,000 whilst a mini-bus was also considered and rejected.

Eventually it was agreed to make gifts to organisations outside the hospital and in order to make sure that the League's charity status was not compromised special permission was obtained from the Charity Commission to do so. The Horsham Mobile Physiotherapy Unit received £500, a TV set was installed at Horsham ambulance station and the main anniversary headline was achieved through a £12,500 gift to the HORACE campaign to equip three ambulances with the latest resuscitation equipment enabling lives to be saved in the home or at the roadside. The hand-over ceremony took place at the annual meeting of May 14, 1984, when The Duchess of Norfolk presented the cheque to HORACE campaigner Dr.David Skipp.

The Vice Chairman of Mid Downs Health Authority, Mrs Lister Williams, praised the League for its "impressive" record, adding that Horsham Hospital was "second to none", trusting that the volunteers would continue to serve for another 25 years.

VIPs AT THE HOSPITAL

ACTOR John Mills brought his whole family to open the fete on June 15, 1971. *(Picture by West Sussex County Times).*

FILM STAR Anthony Andrews at the 1980 summer fete with Molly Andrews. The headline in the local paper read "Andrews meets Andrews".
(Picture by West Sussex County Times).

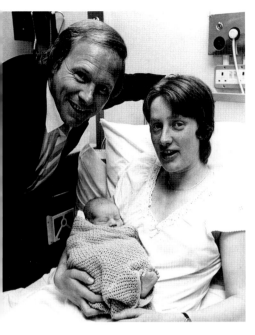

DJ David Hamilton opened the fete in June, 1983, and took time to meet new mother Helen Baines in the maternity unit, with baby Paul.
(Picture by West Sussex County Times).

LORD Tebbit opened the League's fete on May 31, 2008, pictured with Chairman June Smith (left) and Sheila Glaysher.

1984-1985: THE BATTLE TO SAVE MATERNITY IS LOST

THE battle to save the Maternity Unit had been going on since 1978, however it was realised early in 1984 that this much treasured facility was doomed when Mid Downs Health Authority produced a scathing report which described it as "under-used, isolated and inefficient".

This was not an opinion shared with many Horsham mothers or The Community Health Council. Public meetings and banner-waving demonstrations throughout the year illustrated the strength of feeling in the community, campaigners arguing that the Unit was being deliberately under-used so that managers could wind it up.

League members also took a strong stand, keeping up the fight to the bitter end. They had been told that closure would not save money and that the sale of other health properties, Craven Lodge and Beedingwood House, would have paid for necessary modernisations. In October they sent a strongly worded letter to South West Thames Regional Health Authority offering a sum of £30,000 to carry out immediate improvements to the Unit in a last ditch bid to save it. In December Mr.Budd joined a six man delegation to the House of Commons where Health Minister Kenneth Clark had agreed to listen to the town's arguments.

The delegation was kept waiting in an office for a while, then a secretary asked them what questions they planned to ask before eventually ushering them into Mr.Clark's presence. They were all quite shocked to see him sitting behind his desk smoking a cigar, and the day of great expectation fell flat when the Minister said that the closure decision had been taken and there was nothing that he could do about it.

After giving 40 years of service to the town and having thousands of pounds of locally raised funds spent on it, Maternity was closed at the end of March, 1985, the last baby to be born there, Stephanie Etherington. There was a nice touch in the local paper when they published a photograph of mother and baby alongside a picture of the Unit's first baby, Peter Light, born there on April 16, 1945.

"This facility will be sadly missed and I am sure that, as the years pass by and the town continues to grow at a very fast rate, there will become a feeling that the decision was wrong," remarked Mr.Budd in his annual report. With the residents of the town seething, the League sought an urgent meeting with health authority chairman Martyn Long to discuss the whole future of Horsham Hospital.

There was another wet weather disaster for the summer fete, driven inside again, and with concerns about fire risk inside the hospital's tight corridors, the committee set about drawing up contingency plans which might provide alternative cover for a rainy Saturday. They considered underground car parks at the Law Courts, Collyer's School, Horsham Boys Club, the Drill Hall in Denne Road, and looked at insurance cover. Finally they paid £25 to secure the Drill Hall and, clearly fearful about weather prospects, decided to hold the 1985 fete there come rain or shine, a major departure from previous practice.

Two stalwarts stepped down during the year, treasurer Leslie Andrews who had been associated with the committee for 26 years, and secretary Joan Yarborough, however both continued work for the hospital outside the committee with Mrs.Yarborough taking over organization of the shop. Hospital administrator Alan Mills said his goodbyes to be replaced by Peter Holloway.

THE CAMPAIGNING MOTHERS

MOTHERS on the march in 1984 during the long campaign to save Horsham Maternity Unit. In spite of petitions and strong representations by the League, the Unit closed in 1985.
(Picture by West Sussex County Times).

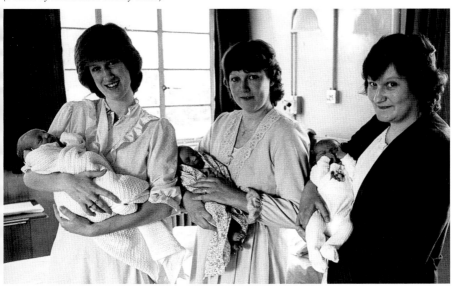

NEW mothers in 1984, Paula Flack, Linda Pullen and Julie Doe, all joined the campaign to save the Unit.
(Picture by West Sussex County Times).

FIRST BABY OF 1945...... AND THE LAST IN 1985

FIRST baby born at Horsham Hospital on April 16, 1945, Peter Light (top left), pictured with members of his family. *(Picture by West Sussex County Times).*

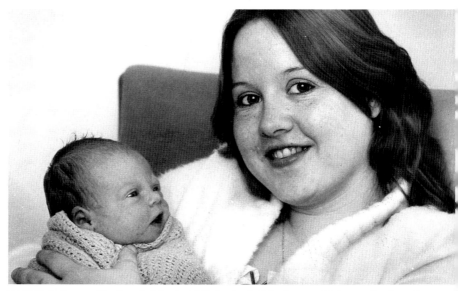

LAST baby born at Horsham in March, 1985, Stephanie Etherington with her mother Lorraine. *(Picture by West Sussex County Times).*

Once more, the League's financial performance was exemplary. There was income of £27,208, the main sums being £8,788 interest, £3,628 donations, £2,935 waste paper, £2,923 subscriptions, £2,540 fete, £2,011 Christmas events, £1,088 tea bar, £983 Private Members Draw, £850 shop. The sale of a small dinghy built in the Occupational Therapy department brought in a welcome £446.

Spending on benevolent services topped £30,000 including the bill for the re-located shop, a sum of £1,008 spent on provision of newspapers and £885 for a long discussed and much needed roadside boundary hedge. Again there was major spending on medical equipment, £24,000 in all, including items for speech therapy, dental, casualty, operating theatre, ante-natal clinic and occupational therapy.

League policy was to do as much as possible to prevent patients having to travel out of town for treatment and this equipment was helping to achieve that along with continuation of minor operations. Chairman Budd reported that he would be calling on Mid Downs to increase the use of Theatre and upgrade Cope and Allcard wards to help in that cause.

The League was in a strong position. It was helping to maintain medical quality through the supply of expensive equipment and it could plan for major projects to come thanks to a policy of saving and building up investments. Even after parting with £30,000, assets early in 1985 stood at £84,000.

The funds were clearly in professional hands, men such as bank manager Budd, accountant Leslie Andrews and auditor Ray Greatorex, who could usually be relied upon to double up as the hospital's Father Christmas.

1985-1986: NEW PSYCHIATRIC WING AND OUT-PATIENTS

FOLLOWING the loss of Maternity and the latest wave of public concern, League officers held several meetings with Chairman Long at Mid Downs in Haywards Heath to ascertain the future of the hospital and in due course they were rewarded with some positive news.

The vacant maternity buildings were to be demolished and replaced by a modern 54 bed Psychiatric Unit which would cater for in-patient and out-patient services following the closure of Roffey Park Hospital in 1984 and the pending closure of St.Christopher's day hospital. This was expected to cost in the region of £3 million with 30 beds for mentally ill, 24 for elderly and a 25 place day centre.

There were also long overdue plans for a "first class" Out Patients Department to cater for 30,000 patients currently using the hospital each year and tentative plans for refurbishment of Cope and Allcard wards.

Later in the year the Friends of Roffey Park and St.Christophers announced that they were winding up and passed on the balance of their funds, £2,319, to the League who agreed to become responsible for the St.Christopher's day centre in Hurst Road.

The Drill Hall summer fete caused some logistical complications, however it made useful profits again, though Mr.Budd reported that "it had lost some of its impact by not being at the hospital" and was pleased the event would return to the hospital in 1986, with the authority agreeing that buildings could be used once more in the event of poor weather.

There was a spate of changes in the committee with former maternity campaigner Shirley Baldwin joining as secretary and the sad death of membership secretary Geoff Counsell whose memory was marked by the purchase of an £860 ECG machine. Three members were moving away from Horsham but active replacements were apparent in the form of Val Winterflood and Maggie Parsons. It was also the year in which a great supporter of the League, Dr John Dew, retired after a distinguished career as a GP.

Income was another all-time record of £31,000, of which the main ingredients were: £9,668 interest, £5,241 waste paper, £3,919 donations, £2,814 subscriptions, £2,264 fete, £1,869 tea bar, £1,364 Christmas events, £1,166 shop, £1,065 Private Members Draw. The committee had also received £479 from sale of Christmas cards, £275 from collecting boxes, £143 raised at a jumble sale and £89 from carol singing.

By comparison with the previous year, the overall spending of £20,444 was quite modest with £13,859 of that being allocated to medical equipment including a £3,527 resectoscope for the Operating Theatre, more eye equipment costing £2,979, bed curtains, electric hoists, treadle fretsaw for Occupational Therapy, an electrocardiograph and a set of baby scales for health visitors. The most costly item under general expenditure was payment of TV rentals at £1,004.

In his annual report Mr. Budd was able to report that the resuscitation equipment purchase for ambulance crews in the previous year had already resulted in the saving of three lives. A very gratifying outcome indeed.

1986-1987: COMMUNITY HOSPITAL FUTURE LOOKS SECURE

THE loss of Maternity had been a big blow to local morale, however Horsham Hospital was beginning to look much more secure with fully functioning geriatric services, 84 beds in Oak, Ash and Beech wards, fully equipped physiotherapy gymnasium, hydrotherapy pool and the John Ingham rehabilitation centre.

Working alongside that in the 1923 buildings were Harvey, Allcard and Cope wards, Casualty Department, Operating Theatre, X-Ray department and well equipped clinics, among them Ante-Natal and Ophthalmology. The 1892 building was also still in constant use, housing all manner of different purposes.

Thanks to new money coming from the sale of Roffey Park, planning was underway to provide a new 72 bed Pyschiatric Unit and a new Out Patients Department which augured well for the future. Managers were also talking about a fully modernized Operating Theatre, expansion of some medical services and redevelopment of many older buildings.

Roy Budd in his 1987 report struck a note of "optimism" declaring that the period of indecision seemed to be over and that at "long last we could look forward to improvements in health services for the people of Horsham." He admitted that Horsham could never aspire to District Hospital status, but as a Community Hospital it would have a special role to play in the care of geriatric and psychiatric patients as well as a variety of other services including GP beds and clinics.

District General Manager Peter Catchpole, addressing the annual meeting, tressed that Horsham would not be devoted entirely to acute medicine for the elderly, though some services would be moving to Crawley, and confirmed that the new buildings were being planned, though these might be three years away.

With the life of the hospital changing, the League also set about changing its own "Objects and Rules" enabling the committee to authorize more donations to outside groups and thus help health services across a wider area. However a suggestion that the League change its name was not implemented.

Because of uncertainties, the League had been allowing its money to grow and at February 1987 total assets stood at a remarkable £100,630. Income for the year was £31,949 with one third of that coming from bank interest whilst huge increases had been derived from the Tea Bar and Waste Paper. The main figures were: Interest £10,765, Subscriptions £3,332, Waste Paper £3,314, Donations £3,252, Fete £2,440, Friends of Roffey Park £2,319, Tea Bar, £1,692, Christmas bazaar £1,687, Private Members Draw £1,136, Shop £895, Cards £600.

Without a "major project", spending was down on the previous year, nevertheless £22,000 went on medical kit, the most significant purchase being £12,000 on field vision equipment to provide another boost for the eye clinic. Allcard received new curtains, physiotherapy "interferential therapy" equipment and Occupational Therapy a micro computer. A mobile lift was also purchased at £1,454.

A newly appointed chaplain was conducting services in what was called The Clubroom in Molly Andrews Way and the League purchased an Irish linen altar cloth at a cost of £57 whilst the question of

providing a proper Chapel continued to be an issue. Proposals for a mini-bus to serve Occupational Therapy was shelved because of difficulty over running costs, but a hospital letter box was provided at £39, and the committee approved extra TV sets for the Royal wedding between Prince Andrew and Sarah Fergusson as well as £300 for ward and staff festivities.

Local authorities were being encouraged to have a bigger involvement in health affairs and early in 1987 Horsham District Council invited the League's Chairman, Treasurer and Secretary to a meeting with senior officers who made it clear that the council would be pressing long term for a brand new hospital whilst in the short term wanted improvements to existing services, especially in the area of Casualty.

1987-1988: HUGE LEGACY AND BIG BOOST FOR X-RAY

THE League's funds were in great shape, made even more so by a windfall legacy of £47,500, the biggest single donation received to date. At about the same time consultant radiologist Dr.Mike Davies made a presentation to the committee demonstrating the urgent need for an Ultra Sound Scanner at Horsham.

With this equipment he believed that it would be possible to prevent up to 1,500 patients from travelling to Crawley each year, including 900 expectant mothers, thus the case was very convincing. This was precisely what the League was in business for and there was no hesitation making the £33,000 purchase and using up part of the legacy.

The status of the X-Ray Department was considerably enhanced and its needs became a continuing priority for the League.

THE X-RAY DEPARTMENT

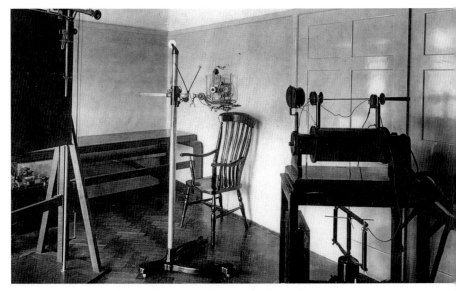

THE introduction of X-Ray at Horsham in 1923 with a very primitive array of equipment.

MORE "modern" equipment being used in the 1940s, with radiographer Miss Martin (right).

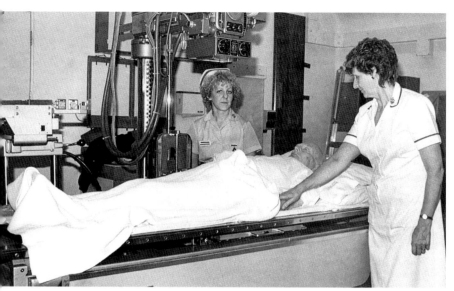

X-RAY work during the 1990's being supervised by Rena Murrell (right)

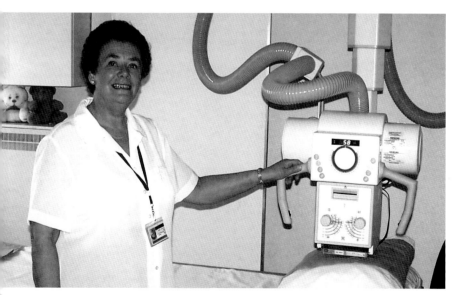

TODAY's X-Ray Department at Horsham has some of the most sophisticated equipment available to the NHS, much of which has been paid for the by the League of Friends. This machine is operated by Vaone Gregory.

A total of £53,372 was spent in the year including £4,740 on mattresses, £2,384 for refurbishment of the Ante Natal Clinic, £1,790 for child psychiatry needs, £1,345 for a staff study room and £1,000 for chiropody.

Under the new rules, donations were also being made outside the hospital with £2,845 given towards grand plans for a post graduate medical centre at Crawley, laser equipment at Crawley and £1,400 to provide car radios for SIMCAS, the Sussex Immediate Medical Care Scheme in which GPs had put themselves on stand-by to attend road accidents and other incidents. The rules were also allowing for gifts to individuals and one of the first was £100 towards an electric wheelchair for a needy patient.

Because of the legacy, there had been an all time record income of £80,126, the other key items being: £14,643 interest, £3,444 fete, £3,139 subscriptions, £2,738 Christmas bazaar, £1,404 waste paper, £1,258 Private Members Draw, £1,237 Tea Bar, £984 Christmas cards, £766 Shop. Assets stood at £123,483.

It was a year dominated by nursing shortages and bed closures affecting the whole region and the League was asked if it could assist with the crisis, perhaps by starting a crèche. There were discussions on taking over part of Forest Hospital for staff use and the formation of a Housing Association to take responsibility whilst urgent help was sought from the district council. The League opted to provide money for the publication of a brochure designed to attract trained staff to join the hospital.

There was a minor hiatus when health managers asked the League to remove its money-spinning waste paper skip from the forecourt, however after talks there was a reprieve, though ominously the issue remained under review.

The manager of what was now called Horsham Health Services, Chris Heppenstall, informed the League that, with the future of the hospital settled, he wished to implement a programme of improvements to the older buildings which would take the hospital through the next 25 years, costing in all around £300,000. The work would involve the merging of Cope and Allcard wards into one common GP ward and improvements to surgery, pharmacy and Harvey Ward.

Mid Downs Health Authority was providing £150,000, however it was thought that the League might front a public fund raising campaign to find the remainder. The committee was left to ponder.

1988-1989: DRAMATIC MOVE TO SAVE OPERATING THEATRE

THE hospital had been doing minor surgery ever since the day it opened in 1892. The new hospital of 1923 included a properly equipped Operating Theatre, it had been thoroughly modernized in 1959 and surgery work continued right through the 1980s and 1990s, saving many patients the need to travel further afield.

Closure was very close in 1988 when staff realized that the operating table was "very many years old" and technicians told them that there were no "spare parts" left on the market, making it redundant. The only way that the Theatre could survive would be through the purchase of a brand new table at £10,000, money that Mid Downs Health Authority did not have.

The League committee view was that the NHS should provide basic equipment of this nature however they drew the conclusion that if the Theatre was closed, even temporarily, it would be "lost forever to

Horsham" and so they came up with the ingenious idea to loan Mid Downs the money, repayable in the next financial year. The deal was done, the table was purchased immediately and the surgery list continued.

There was another big plus for medical work when the League purchased a £12,000 Auto Refractor for the Eye Clinic, one of the first of its type in the country which provided patients with a visual and printed prescription for glasses following a two minute test. "A lot of eye patients are senior citizens and from April 1 tests will be subject to a charge. It was therefore a must for Horsham," commented the Chairman.This proved another major asset for one of the best equipped eye clinics in the region.

The spending list for the year came out at £79,000, including the bill for the Ultrasound Scanner from the previous year, whilst £4,845 was spent on beds, £4,840 on a laryngoscopy system for the Ear Nose and Throat Clinic, £3,839 on a photo-copier and £2,107 on refurbishments for Astonleigh nurses home and Out Patients.

The outgoings were much higher than the income of £42,495, however with assets remaining at £129,496 this was not of any concern. Because the old maternity building was being demolished and builders were at work on the new Psychiatric Wing, the summer fete was forced back to the Drill Hall again yet still managed to make £3,276. Both Tea Bar and Shop were thriving under the leadership of Gwen Tilling and Joan Yarborough, realizing £1,802 and £1,384 respectively, whilst bank interest brought in £13,837 and donations and legacies £11,025.

Other significant sums included: £3,295 subscriptions, £3,059 Christmas bazaar, £3,083 Waste Paper, £1,198 Private Members Draw and collecting boxes £467. Profit on Christmas cards was down to just

£69 but a bundle of old stock numbering 5,000 cards had been found in a cupboard and action was being taken to sell these next year.

A special sub committee was set up to see if shop profits could be raised, however, after making detailed enquiries, members reported back to say that the shop was performing really well. There was a serious problem being created in the hospital foyer which staff often found scattered with discarded cigarette ends. It was the League who stepped in to resolve the problem by purchasing two large bins.

The long serving Leslie Andrews, who had been the first auditor in 1959, had done a long stint as treasurer and proved a valuable committee member too, stepped down from active duty after clocking up nearly 30 years service. Even then, he continued to provide support by taking care of the League's important covenanted subscriptions. Apart from the Patron, Leslie held the record as the longest survivor of the launch committee.

LAVINIA the Duchess of Norfolk, League patron for 36 years.

THE COMMUNITY HOSPITAL 1989

STAFF representing several departments pose for a publicity brochure financed by the League in 1989. The Sister in the centre is Chris Lancaster.

A focal point of hospital life, the Tea Bar and Shop, pictured prior to a major redesign of the shop in 1997.

ONE of the garden courtyards provided by the League.

A volunteer helps a patient with flower arranging.

Friends of the Hospital: 1989-1998

Centenary and growth of specialist clinics

1989-1990: CAMPAIGN TO IMPROVE CONDITIONS

ANXIETY over the future of the hospital was never far away. It emerged again in 1989 at a time when millions of NHS money was being diverted into the new Princess Royal Hospital at Haywards Heath, a flagship project undertaken by Mid Downs Health Authority.

Horsham was struggling to make do with a temporary Out Patients Department housed in a prefabricated building, there was continuing demand for better Casualty services whilst the opening of the new Mental Health Unit had been delayed.

The League took a very bold step by joining forces with the West Sussex County Times to launch the "Help Horsham Hospital" campaign which lasted several months and attracted much public attention including the signing of a petition by 25,000 residents duly delivered direct to Margaret Thatcher at 10, Downing Street.

Armed with this support, a League delegation confronted the Chairman of Mid Downs, Martyn Long, at a "frank and helpful" meeting on the current financial situation. They were told that Horsham had been allocated £3 million from the sale of Roffey Park for the Mental Health Unit, due to open in 1990, but that no money was available to improve Casualty or replace the over burdened Out Patients.

Chairman Budd told the annual meeting that the best that Horsham could hope for

was a new study into the future of Out Patients, but regretfully he believed that the chance of ever having a proper emergency service could not be fulfilled. "I am sorry to say that it has always been apparent, and more so in the 90s, that the money is just not available for this to happen."

Whilst the fabric of the buildings was crumbling in parts, the hospital continued to have some of the best equipment available to the health service thanks in no small measure to the work of the Friends.

As the League came to the end of its 30th year, the shape of the committee looked like this: Chairman, Roy Budd; Vice Chairman, Mrs.D.J.Yarborough; Secretary, George Peet; Treasurer, Mr.Michael Bennett; Membership Secretary, Val Winterflood; Legal Adviser, Ken Bentall; Auditors, Hodgson Impey; other committee members, Mrs.M.Nunn, Mrs.M.Parsons, Mr.L.Brooks, Miss D.Harber, Mrs.E.M.Joy.

The energy of the now well established charitable body was not faltering. Income exceeded £50,000, thanks mainly to bank interest of £16,870, donations of £12,640, waste paper £4,804, subscriptions £4,021, summer fete £4,016 and Christmas bazaar £2,464, along with strong contributions from tea bar, shop, private members draw and collecting boxes.

More than £22,000 was spent, the largest item being resuscitation equipment worth £6,288 for Out Patients. Other sums went on a £1,700 cot death monitor, a staff recruitment brochure costing £1,800, staff sitting room improvements at £2,962, window blinds £2,815, and a Pegasus airwave bed £2,480. Proceeds from the council's Civic Ball were also received and spent on a laser unit for Physiotherapy.

Because of "uncertainty" over the future direction of services at Horsham, the League did not commit to major projects at this time and the balance sheet revealed judicious investments by the Treasurer in a variety of banks, building societies and savings accounts which showed total assets of £154,478. The League was becoming quite wealthy and well placed to deal with major needs in the future.

1990-1991: ROY BUDD STEPS DOWN AFTER 11 YEARS

THERE had been only three Chairman in the League's first 30 years and the third of these, Roy Budd, had completed eleven years service when announcing his retirement at the annual meeting of May 21, 1990. In his farewell remarks he mentioned that efforts to persuade managers to improve Out Patients had not progressed, however he was leaving a League of Friends functioning in great shape.

On a hopeful note, unit manager Neil Zammett told the same meeting that there would be "no further reductions" at Horsham whilst the Mental Health Unit would open in April, 1991.

Once again no major projects were undertaken and incoming chairman George Peet reported "a reasonably quiet year" in his 1991 report, though this quiet time had resulted in the spending of no less than £30,400 on amenities. The largest of these was the up-grading of Harvey Ward toilets at £7,760 whilst a processor for X-Ray cost £3,881, specialist equipment for testing children's hearing £1,805, two new beds £1,771, and a miscellaneous list of other items took up £3,900. A sum of £2,049 had also been spent on improving gardens, a donation of £3,000 made towards cataract operations and £2,700 given towards nurse training.

As regular fund raising activities continued to thrive, bank interest grew and more donations and legacies poured in, a familiar pattern of income exceeding expenditure emerged. Total income amounted to £63,375 of which £22,311 was derived from gifts and an enormous £21,658 received in the form of interest. Other significant sums came via subscriptions £4,941, fete £4,316 and bazaar £2,668, and the ever reliable tea bar, shop, private members draw and waste paper.

The lucrative waste paper business was about to vanish, however, as a new home had to be found for the ugly skip occupying car park space and after some tentative efforts to get things going elsewhere the whole enterprise was handed over to the district council's recycling programme. The committee soon found a new source of funds through the first "flag day" collection held in Swan Walk which brought in £538, thereafter repeated each October.

Treasurer Michael Bennett was indeed a happy man. The League's very successful investment policy had resulted in deposits of £79,000 with building societies, £61,383 with National Savings, and £19,264 with Government stocks, giving total assets at February 28, 1991, of £183,152.

1991-1992: IMPROVEMENTS FOR CASUALTY DEPARTMENT

THE League was not just a fund-raising organisation, it was an association of people who cared about the hospital and local health services. George Peet took up that theme in his report of May 20, 1991, explaining what a difference the League was making to day-to-day life at the hospital by providing such things as newspapers for the wards, the renting of TV sets, public telephones, fish tanks, the shop and tea bar.

The latest venture was a book trolley in reception launched by Maggie Parsons and a team of helpers providing both a service and income too.

He was concerned about dropping membership, now down to 1,475, and called for younger people to come forward. There was continuing concern about the lack of action to improve Out Patients, though the opening date for the new Rose Ward providing for 14 psychiatric patients had been fixed for that summer.

There was much sadness in the next year when Mr.Peet died, having served six years as secretary and then chairman. The committee devoted renewed attention to the ailing Casualty Department and with money given in the memory of the late Chairman coupled with League funds they paid for the complete refurbishment of the reception area, costing in all £16,280, whilst Horsham Lions came forward with a further £10,000 to improve conditions for patients using that busy department.

This was a much needed boost for the department which the NHS could not provide.

At the annual meeting of May 11, 1992, new chairman Mrs. Joan Yarborough, with Maggie Parsons as her Vice Chairman and Joy Joy secretary, had the task of summing up another remarkable year of fund-raising, total income being £86,277. Legacies and donations had brought in £42,343, interest £20,712, subscriptions £5,525, fete £4,492, bazaar £3,347 whilst the newer ventures, town collection and bookstall made £972 and £750. Tea bar, shop, Christmas cards and members draw all topped £1,000 profits.

There were two big purchases, a dental X-Ray machine at £9,520 and an ultra-sound scanner for Ante Natal at £7,995, along with beds and mattresses, a pulse oximeter for the wards and a plaster cast saw for Out Patients. The committee also financed new vending machines needed to comply with EEC regulations, refurbishment of the nurses' home at Astonleigh, various items of furniture, office equipment and training materials and a donation to the emergency doctor service, totalling in all £36,795.

Once more behind the scenes the health service structure was changing and the League was told how hospitals at Horsham and Crawley would operate under a single manager based at Crawley in preparation for the creation of the new Crawley Horsham NHS Trust.

1992-1993: HOSPITAL CELEBRATES THE CENTENARY

THERE was good cause for celebration in the July of 1992 when Horsham Hospital marked its centenary and the fore-fathers of the great enterprise were duly remembered.

The centre-piece was an exhibition of historic photographs and equipment, with League members acting as hosts, attended by 500 schoolchildren. Around 350 staff and their partners attended a garden party on July 4 when the Duchess of Norfolk planted an ornamental pear tree and a cake was cut by the Chairman of Horsham District Council Jean Burnham. There was also a thanksgiving service at the parish church, and a nurses' reunion, whilst the League sponsored souvenirs and paid to have photographs and documents framed for permanent display. This included a brief, but beautifully hand lettered, history extracted from The Horsham Hospital Book assembled in 1923, and given pride of place in reception at a presentation conducted by Mrs.Yarborough.

It was a momentous year in more than one respect for the Friends broke all previous records by raising an amazing total of £138,000. This was truly exceptional, boosted mainly by legacies of £84,699. Nevertheless lots of hard work had been done to raise £5,219 at the fete, blessed by fine weather, and £3,694 at the Christmas bazaar now being run from the hospital foyer. Other sums included £22,702 interest, £5,334 subscriptions and a significant £2,430 from the tea bar.

In her report of May 17, 1993, Mrs. Yarborough was able to point to spending of £54,000, a large part of which went to settle the bill for the newly refurbished Casualty Department, now proving of great benefit to patients and staff alike. Other expensive purchases included an ENT microscope at £4,837, a steriliser for the operating theatre £3,912, trolleys for day surgery £3,164, an ECG machine for Lilac and Rose wards £1,315 and four hoists for the wards £2,596. Again the committee invested several thousands in staff training and a range of miscellaneous items including four two way radios, ten pocket memos, word processor for the Health Community Centre and another donation for mobile physiotherapy work.

There could be little doubt that Horsham Hospital in its centenary year was being propped up by volunteers in much the same tradition as the 1892 forbears.

One of the busiest jobs was that being undertaken by the treasurer who was now managing funds in two building societies, two bank accounts, National Savings, and Government stocks. Centenary year presented him with another enormous surplus of £94,784 which, at February 28, 1993, brought assets up to £311,000.

The League was in a unique position of strength, ready to respond to a major project at short notice.

1993-1994: HORSHAM TO BECOME 'PREMIER HOSPITAL'

A NEW era dawned in 1993 with the launch of Crawley Horsham NHS Trust devoted exclusively to the needs of hospitals at Crawley and Horsham, chaired by Dr.Tony Martin, the doctor who had supervised geriatric services at Horsham's new wing in 1981.

At the League's annual meeting on May 17, 1993, Dr Martin explained the new concept of Trusts being the "provider" of health services and GP Fund Holders being the "purchasers", with doctors acting accordingly to meet the needs of patients.

More importantly he announced that the Trust's target was to make Horsham Hospital "a Premier Community Hospital" and that plans were already in hand to create a dedicated GP Unit at the hospital whilst a new Out Patient Department would be built, with £1.2 million available to spend during 1994. An appeal had also been launched to purchase a state of the art Scanner to benefit patients at both hospitals.

All this was music to the ears of the League. Members had been pressing for hospital improvements since 1989 and this was the signal to begin a new phase of serious expenditure. Mrs.Yarborough announced that the capital reserve fund of £225,000 would be devoted to provide furnishings and equipment for the new ventures, Out Patients and GP Unit.

As a bonus, the committee went ahead immediately with the spending of £38,000 to upgrade the main reception, waiting area and tea-bar. This was a considerable undertaking involving installation of automatic sliding doors for better public access, new lighting, sofas, chairs, coffee tables, carpets and curtains. Early plans included a "welcome hostess desk" however

HOSPITAL CENTENARY 1992

THE hospital's centenary was marked in 1992 when Chairman Joan Yarborough presented this framed history, received by Dr Tony Martin, for display in reception.

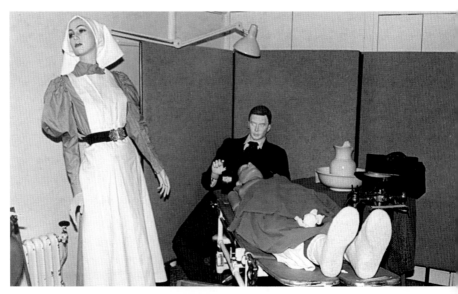

ONE of the displays at the centenary exhibition.

THE Duchess of Norfolk plants a tree in the hospital gardens.

THE centenary cake is cut by Horsham Council Chairman Jean Burnham.

this was dropped in favour of a volunteer doing duty at the main entrance. The Friends were delighted by the work, officially unveiled by Mrs.Yarborough.

Treasurer Michael Bennett reported that assets had grown by 37 per cent, though he urged some caution because the abnormal growth had been mainly due to exceptionally high legacies. Nevertheless, he welcomed the new department which would enable the League "to divest themselves of a considerable amount of capital and thereby deflect some criticism concerning the 'hoarding' of monies". He pointed out that, if assets were reduced by £200,000, total annual income would fall to around £40,000, a figure lower than the normal expenditure of recent years.

It was unlikely that the League would match the £138,000 raised in 1993. However the 1994 figure was an impressive £69,000 with more good weather resulting in a magnificent £5,180 from the summer fete, a contribution of £3,138 from the Christmas bazaar and a street collection of £825, with book trolley, shop and tea bar, all making significant contributions.

Of that, £56,000 was spent on hospital amenities, the largest portion being £38,000 devoted to the enhancement of reception, waiting area and tea bar. Other gifts included improvements to the Ante Natal Clinic at £1,087, a Lees Screen £1,608, hoists and slings £1,640, ear testing equipment £3,000, a plaster saw £1,360 and numerous smaller items.

The Chairman encouraged a new drive for members by circulating letters to all houses on the North Horsham estates whilst a number of talks on the role of the League were given to various organisations, these efforts resulting in steady growth and a figure of 1,500 subscribers. It was a year of "very satisfactory accomplishment" with promise of some bigger achievements to come.

Meeting with the volunteers, Trust Chief Executive Graham Elderfield confirmed that Horsham would get a new purpose-built Out Patient department and a new GP Unit, however there was some concern when he announced that a working party had been set up to look into the future running of what was now being called The Minor Injuries Unit.

The League was very wary about this and sent off a letter to Mr.Elderfield making the position quite clear. "The people of Horsham have contributed a vast amount of money for Horsham Hospital to preserve and improve facilities. As you know, £225,000 has been set aside for equipping the new Out Patients Department and £25,000 for the opening of a dedicated GP Unit. All this, together with the rising population and increased housing, has made us decide that we are unable to support anything less than the Minor Injuries Unit service we now have with a doctor in attendance."

The Unit survived with its Monday to Friday, 9-5 format, though there was a significant change when the highly regarded medical officer Dr.Suresh Dewan was, on his retirement, replaced by a new generation of highly trained Nurse Practitioners.

1994-1995: BIG DONATION SAVES DAY SURGICAL WORK

THE operating theatre had been built in 1923 and the League had stepped in more than once to provide it with vital equipment, thus preventing closure. It was evident again in 1994 that equipment was falling well below required standards and the theatre was being under-used to the extent that it was again threatened.

The Trust came up with proposals to purchase £87,000's worth of new equipment for a range of ENT, gynaecology and general surgery such as hernias, varicose veins, vasectomies and in-growing toe nails to be dealt with at Horsham. The town's doctors were in favour, Park Surgery producing £32,000 and the League giving a substantial sum of £53,000. The League committee, however, was getting tough. It imposed three conditions: 1) that all the new equipment remained at Horsham, 2) that all items be clearly marked League of Friends, Horsham, and 3) All staff who had been transferred to Crawley should be allowed to return to Horsham Hospital Theatre, if they so desired.

The enterprise meant that many more patients could be treated at Horsham, waiting lists were cut in both towns and some much needed activity was restored to the Horsham theatre which continued functioning for several more years to come.

The long serving Joan Yarborough stepped down as Chairman after completing a three year stint and tributes were paid to her sterling work over many years which had included launching the first tea bar in 1976 and running the shop for a period of 14 years.

Work had begun on combining the former women's ward Allcard with the children's ward Cope to form a new dedicated GP Unit in which local doctors could treat their patients and in her final report of May 16, 1994, Mrs.Yarborough revealed that a sum of £32,000 would be dedicated to this work, including provision of a nurse call system, desks, chairs, vinyl flooring and curtaining. Horsham District Council bought ten chairs costing £1,500 and the Unit became

operational that November whilst a further £2,200 was spent on curtaining Ash, Beech and Oak wards.

The treasurer reported assets up from £311,000 to £324,000, but pointed out that £225,000 had been earmarked for the new Out Patients Department, currently in the planning stage, and that once current major projects had been completed the League would be operating at a different level, precluding any major projects for some time.

Incoming Chairman, Mrs.Maggie Parsons, in her first report on May 15, 1995, confirmed that after the spending of £53,000 on day surgery, the League had set aside £170,000 for the new Out Patients, due to be functioning in 1996, and a "shopping list" had been asked for. She had much to say about the "new ways" of the NHS, regretting the loss of Matrons and was especially unhappy that Ward Sisters were now being called Ward Managers.

Fund raising brought in £69,968 with a weather hit fete making £4,354, Christmas bazaar £3,383, and town collection £844 "proving that the people of Horsham love and support their hospital" remarked Mrs.Parsons. Legacies and donations amounted to a very significant £27,795, interest £19,398, subscriptions £5,401, tea bar £3,301, shop £3,234 and members draw £1,060. The treasurer lamented the "final disappearance" of income from waste paper sales but believed that the loss had been compensated for.

Nearly all of this was spent, on the GP Unit, new curtaining and a range of smaller items including toys and books for use by children in the reception area, thus very little was transferred into the League's investment portfolio. Nevertheless, at February 1995, total assets remained at £320,320.

1995-1996: PATRON SERVED LEAGUE FOR 36 YEARS

THE Death of Lavinia, Duchess of Norfolk, was recorded with great sadness and a group of members attended a service of thanksgiving at Arundel Cathedral on March 1, 1995.

The Duchess had been appointed Patron soon after the formation of the League in 1959 and for 36 years had been a great supporter and source of inspiration, working with six different chairmen and a host of changing committee members. Links with the Norfolks were maintained when her daughter, The Lady Mary Mumford, agreed to assume the role.

At last the long awaited Out Patient building came into sight. As the foundations of the £1.2 million building were being laid and a 14 month building programme started, the committee was heartened to learn through a new policy document Developing Health Services in the Horsham District that a range of extra clinics was being planned. There was approval all-round for sketch plans and over a period of several months dozens of items were purchased in readiness.

Biggest expenditure linked to Out Patients was an Ultrasound Scanner costing £49,950 placed in X-Ray. This was to prove vital to the working of the new clinics enabling many more patients being seen at Horsham rather than Crawley. At the same time, £34,459 was spent on the complete re-flooring of Oak, Ash and Beech wards replacing carpets that were more than 14 years old.

Mrs. Yarborough finally gave up control of the shop, handing over to Doug Hartman, June Smith was among new committee members and Val Winterflood was thanked for completing a ten year stint as membership secretary. The ever busy Geoff Matthews organised a musical concert for patients in the John Ingham Unit, appreciated by the occupational therapists.

News came through that the planned Postgraduate Medical Centre at Crawley would not be built and the League's donation of £2,845 was being returned, though members agreed to transfer this to equipment instead. It was also discovered that Crawley was "borrowing" equipment from Horsham and the committee asked that written permission be obtained before this was done.

There was some dismay when the Horsham switchboard was moved permanently to Crawley leaving no-one on reception out of hours though, with growing pressures from increased users, it was deemed more efficient to centralise this work.

It was another good year for income, a total of £62,940 received, thanks to the League's mainstays: £19,462 interest, £18,197 donations and legacies, £5,718 subscriptions, £5,195 fete and £1,209 draw. The tea bar contributed a remarkable £4,036, shop £3,474 and collection at Tesco £711, with other sums from collection boxes, Christmas cards and bookstall. Lady Mary joined helpers in running another successful Christmas bazaar which raised £3,404.

Spending on small items came to a rather modest £17,821, though a further £38,090 had been taken from reserves for the Day Surgery project making the year's outlay £55,911, and leaving assets in hand of £327,349. A sum of £235 was donated to provide resuscitation mannequins for the training of all staff and the committee was given a demonstration on how lives could be saved, particularly through the removal of throat obstructions.

It was often a roller-coaster ride for the committee. One minute approving spending of thousands on sophisticated medical equipment such as a Hitachi Scanner, the next deciding what to spend on fish food or fixing a leaky tea bar boiler. Each year gifts of all shapes and sizes were received, some that could be sold and turned into useful money, others that could be utilised. Among the most unusual was 30 prize carp for the garden ponds.

1996-1997: NEW OUT PATIENTS DEPARTMENT OPENED

CONSULTANTS had been visiting Horsham Hospital since the Second World War and regular clinics established, however many of these had soldiered on in sub-standard rooms, including the old 1892 buildings and prefabricated structures.

The League was at the forefront of calling for a purpose built Out Patient Department and now, after eight years of planning, the job was complete. Architects had fitted the building very neatly into a void between the main reception area and X-Ray building, complete with its own entrance and grand waiting area. It was an extremely important step in securing the future of the hospital and ensured that many thousands of patients could be seen by specialists in their home town in warm and comfortable surroundings.

Speaking at the annual meeting on May 12, Mrs. Parsons said that Horsham people were "very proud of their hospital and guarded it well". Following the sad death of Michael Bennett, the post of treasurer was taken over by Bob Butler with Reu Brown assuming responsibility for covenanted subscriptions. Residents had every right to be very proud of the finished Out Patient Department, commented Mr.Butler. He

added that the League's promise to spend £225,000 had been fulfilled on equipment, furniture and a range of support items, including X-Ray services essential to the purpose of diagnosis, paid in various sums spread out over three years. Thanks for the League's "tremendous generosity" were given by Trust chairman Dr.Martin.

The official opening was performed on June 14, 1997 by Lady Mary Mumford, and committee member Mr.I.R.Philp summed up feelings when he commented: "The new department is something for people to see as a very concrete commitment that the Trust is committing itself to Horsham Hospital. Everyone knows that it is here to stay."

A plaque was erected in reception stating that thanks to "generous donations made by many in the Horsham district" £216,000 had been donated to the hospital between 1995 and 1998, of which £120,000 had been devoted to the Out Patient building.

League spending soared to £101,887 that year with £37,781 devoted to equipment, £57,988 on scanner plus peripheral X-Ray needs and £6,118 on routine services, a new record. Minor Injuries was given £2,628 for computers to help manage the flow of 9,007 patients who passed through in 1996, including 2,944 children.

Income for the year was down slightly to £51,160, but now the League was rightly dipping into reserves that it had so carefully built up over a period of years. Interest, donations and subscriptions brought in the usual big sums whilst fund-raising produced in all £22,170, led by the fete £6,124, tea bar £5,481, bazaar £4,264, shop £2,702 and draw £1,260.

With thousands of patients using Out Patients and Minor Injuries, continuation of day surgery, fully functional wards and psychiatric wing, the hospital was

OUT PATIENTS DEPARTMENT

THE modern Out Patients Department opened by League Patron, Lady Mary Mumford, on June 14, 1997. The League gave £120,000 towards fitting out the department and has a proud record of supporting many clinics.

THE comfortable reception area in the Out Patients Department.

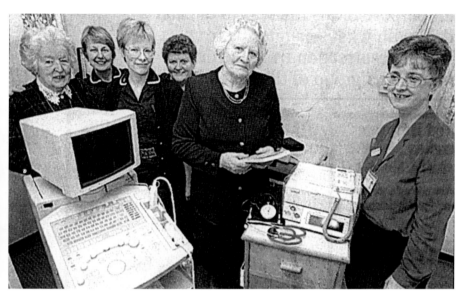

EQUIPMENT for the Ante Natal section costing £35,000 was presented in 1998. Pictured are Joy Joy, Carol Fry, Trish Church, Ann O'Donoghue, Maggie Parsons and Eileen Nolan.
(Picture by West Sussex County Times).

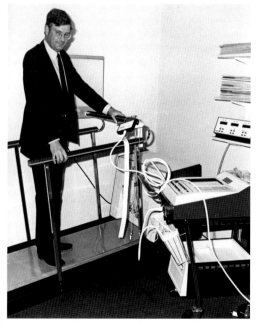

HEART monitoring and blood pressure equipment costing £6,000 given by the League, being tested here by Dr Tony Martin.

progressing. However, life in the NHS does not remain still for long. Early in 1996 the League learned that another "consultation" phase was beginning with launch of a Patient Care Review undertaken by West Sussex Health Authority and the Eastern Surrey Health Commission on the future of Crawley and Horsham NHS Trust and its neighbouring East Surrey Healthcare NHS Trust.

Somewhat ominously members were told that "the status quo was not in the best interests of patients and some change is needed over the next five years". It became obvious that these plans were going to have major implications for services to Horsham patients.

1997-1998: CHAPEL AND 'NEW LOOK' SHOP COMPLETED

TWIN projects emerged when hospital staff moved to provide a long yearned for Chapel whilst the League decided to tackle the much discussed question of upgrading the Shop.

Trust Director of Nursing Veronica James, a regular at meetings, informed the committee that Horsham was among the few hospitals without a Chapel and that plans were being made to provide one by extending the existing clubroom and converting a bar area into a small room for clergy. It would be inter-denominational, there would be wheelchair access and the cost would be £50,000.

The League started the Chapel Fund rolling with £5,000 and staff became very busy organising fund raisers, including a successful car wash in the X-Ray car park. When £10,000 had been achieved application was made for Trust money, however, later in the year the Chaplain, the Reverend Gordon

Skipp, announced with delight that he had received an anonymous £50,000 cheque to get the job done without further delay. It was agreed that the League's donation would be used for a specific item.

The Chapel of St.Luke, with specially commissioned windows depicting healing, light and hope, was dedicated on May 20, 1998, at a service attended by the Roman Catholic Bishop of Arundel and Brighton, the Anglican Bishop of Horsham and the General Secretary of the Free Churches Council, welcomed by Trust Chief Executive Isabel Gowan.

This was a very significant step for the hospital. An early Chapel from the 1930s had disappeared and more than 30 years previously the League had opened a Chapel fund which, amid controversy and development delays, had been abandoned and money diverted elsewhere.

The need to improve and enlarge the shop for increasing numbers of patients and visitors had been discussed for years and a special sub committee devoted many hours before presenting a scheme for complete relocation along with ambitious ideas for a conservatory and patio. The latter were dropped on cost grounds, however the new look shop was built on empty land just behind the old one at a final price of £38,065.

Mrs.Parsons, who had spent time in Allcard Ward as a patient following an appendix operation, thanked everyone for their good humour in dealing with the dust and noise caused by the alterations, announcing that a Shop Trolley had been launched to go around the wards twice a week.

Following the major spending, bank interest declined accordingly with total income down to £45,526 whilst general

THE hospital's Chapel of St.Luke was dedicated in 1998 and built thanks to an anonymous donation of £50,000 plus £5,000 from staff fund raising and £5,000 from the League. The stained glass windows depict healing, light and hope.

AN earlier Chapel in the 1923 building was used for many years and mentioned in an inventory carried out in 1934. It closed to make room for a modernised X-Ray department.

expenditure around the hospital dropped to a new low of just £15,563, the most significant item being new furniture for the committee room at £3,432. The bulk of incoming money came from donations and subscriptions of £10,209 and fund raising efforts which realised £23,859. The fete was a continuing success at £6,192 whilst tea bar had rocketed to £6,040, bazaar £4,035, shop £3,592 and draw £1,131. Other significant sums came from telephones £947, collection £650, books £526, cards £513 and boxes £233.

The remaining commitment to equip the new Out Patients Department amounting to £112,690 was drawn from reserves, making total outgoings a very significant sum of £128,563, which Bob Butler called "a record indeed". Total assets had slipped to £200,462, but this was still a healthy position.

There were some embarrassing moments at the May 11 annual meeting when the hospital alarm system triggered twice during a talk on psychiatric services given by Sir Patrick Symons. Later in the meeting the Chairman awarded a special badge to retiring Trust chairman Dr.Tony Martin who for many years had worked for the good of the hospital and had given the League "a great deal of support and understanding".

Dr Martin responded by saying that Horsham had one of the best Leagues in the country and that it was a privilege to accept life membership.

Change was much in the air again and the League was coming to terms with another new administration when Crawley/Horsham Trust was merged with East Surrey Trust, to form Sussex and Surrey Healthcare NHS Trust. Matters were further complicated when the psychiatric wing was transferred to the new Chichester Priority Care Trust, later to become Sussex Weald and Downs Trust,

now called Sussex Partnership NHS Foundation Trust. Inevitably, with each new regime the dust took a long time to settle.

The League was concerned that Horsham did not have a designated "hospital manager" and sent off a missive to regional health bosses seeking action. Eventually a reply was received pointing out that there were many senior members of staff present including ward managers, a site services manager and heads of department.

However, the League committee was not convinced, yearning no doubt for the old days of Matron, Hospital Secretary and the House Committee.

There were further fears about Horsham equipment being moved to other hospitals along with staff and the committee asked that all items purchased by the League should be clearly marked League of Friends, Horsham. Managers agreed, though it was not a practice that endured.

1998-1999: 50TH ANNIVERSARY OF NATIONAL LEAGUE

DURING its 50th year the National League of Hospital Friends came up with a new title to focus on a wider field of voluntary work, becoming the National Association of Hospital and Community Friends.

Horsham had been a member for 40 of those years and planned a £50,000 spending programme with some new benefits for the Ante Natal Clinic, Physiotherapy and Hydrotherapy and general improvements to floors. The year was also marked by an official visit from the association's South East Chairman Mrs Ann Caffyn who toured the hospital with Lady Mary.

Income amounted to £53,344 with

£26,245 coming from fund raising work, the summer fete topping the table with £6,285 followed by the highly successful tea bar at £6,075, shop £4,897, bazaar £4,273, draw £1,299 and telephones £1,181. Spending came to £48,426, the bulk of which settled the bill for the shop re-building project with some smaller spending on tea bar, baby clinic, leg ulcer clinic and some "propulse ear irrigators".

After a period of major spending on Day Surgery, new Out Patient Department and scanner for X-Ray, treasurer Mr.Butler expected a return to "more normal" levels of spending in future. He anticipated regular income of around £50,000 of which £10,000 was committed to various annual services, including TV rentals, provision of newspapers and maintenance of vending machines, leaving £40,000 for new equipment.

Assets levelled off at £205,000, producing a very useful £11,000 a year interest, whilst Mr.Butler believed that any future special projects would have to rely on legacy income, which naturally varied from year to year. His vision soon came true. During the next few years the League received huge injections of money through some remarkable gifts.

At the annual meeting of May 17, 1999, chairman Mrs.Parsons thanked Joy Napper for eight years of hard work running the tea bar, chasing up lost tea cups, dealing with leaky boilers and constantly having to find change for £20 notes. The Tea Bar had evolved into one of the League's most effective fund raising activities and the Chairman was pleased to welcome in a new team of organisers, Carolyn Dodd and Margaret Butcher.

In the 50th year of the NHS and the League's 40th things were going well for the voluntary helpers of the hospital, much achieved and money still in the bank.

However, there was a whirlwind of activity going on within the Health Service. Yet another new administrative body arrived on the scene with the emergence of Horsham and Chanctonbury Primary Care Group based at Park House.

At meetings with the committee, PCG chairman Dr. Jace Clarke announced that Horsham Hospital was "under used and under developed" whilst chief officer Angela Ugur added that a "thorough appraisal" of the hospital was about to take place.

All this coincided with the Patient Care Review launched by West Sussex Health Authority which generated immense public disquiet, for at its core was the proposed transfer of Accident and Emergency and Maternity from Crawley Hospital to East Surrey Hospital.

Worried committee members received assurances from Director of Nursing Shona Brown that Horsham's future was safe, however there was intense concern about the extended travel that emergency patients would face going to Redhill, especially expectant mothers. In the previous year 600 babies from Horsham had been born at Crawley and it had not been forgotten that when Horsham maternity closed promises had been made about mothers receiving "top level" services nearby, at Crawley.

As Chairman Mrs.Parsons remarked at the annual meeting, "there was a great deal of anxiety about the future of our hospital."

THE tea bar has become one of the League's foremost fund raisers, organised by Margaret Butcher (right) and Carolyn Dodd (left) and a big team of enthusiastic volunteers including above Joan Carter and Yvonne Scarry.

BOOK sales bring in large sums each year thanks to the work of volunteers. Pictured are Audrey and Geoff Matthews who supervised the project for many years.

ANOTHER source of income is the League's hospital shop which was rebuilt in 1998 at a cost of £38,000. Many volunteers are required to keep it going, among them above Bryan Thompson, Elsie Lee and Joyce Panter.

AN earlier and much smaller shop provided after building of the new wing in 1981.

Friends of the Hospital: 1999-2008

Big spending heralds new future for the Hospital

1999-2000: LEGACY PROVIDES NEW COURTYARD GARDEN

LEGACIES and donations in the memory of loved ones had contributed much to funds ever since the start, were greatly appreciated and well used. The contribution received early in 1999 was out of the ordinary in that the late Mrs Ruby V.Rylatt had left her house, its contents and her bank account to the League of Friends.

The committee found itself in the unusual position of owning a domestic home and a team of members spent time assessing and distributing the contents to various fund raising causes before the property was sold for £90,000. Some items went for auction including a rare box of hatpins.

It was decided to dedicate The Courtyard Garden project to the memory of the generous donor and a landscaper was brought in to help transform a previously run down area into a highly pleasing garden with shrubbery, paths, water feature and comfortable seating, complete with a plaque in memory of Mrs.Rylatt. The venture cost £24,000 and the opening ceremony was performed after the annual meeting of May 16, 2000, by Dr.Richard Bailey. The Courtyard quickly became very popular with patients, visitors and staff alike, particularly on fine days.

This event marked the conclusion of a series of works involving complete refurbishment of the main entrance, reception, seating areas, shop, tea bar, and now gardens, something that Chairman Mrs.Parsons was very proud of.

Because of the exceptional windfall, income for the year soared to £145,750, the legacy realising in total £96,571. A further £26,454 had come from fund raising with tea bar now top of the league at £6,740, fete £6,159, shop £5,479, bazaar £4,192, members draw £1,343, with significant sums from collections, greetings cards, books and telephones. Among donations were 30 copies of a local poetry book which the League was invited to sell at £3 each.

Due to the large injection of money, other projects came rapidly. The Ante Natal Clinic received a scanner, a heart rate monitor and foetal detector, costing £34,361, these proving a great boon to midwives and reducing travel for expectant mums. The whole of Molly Andrews Way was provided with noise free floor covering along with porters lodge, staff canteen and Child Development Clinic at £9,990. The tea bar got a £7,004 facelift to complement the recently improved seating area and to meet new health standards, whilst curtains were provided for Physiotherapy and Hydrotherapy at £1,549.

Spending in this remarkable year amounted to £81,893, many projects planned in the anniversary year completed and paid for.

As the League began its fifth decade it faced the future with a strong team: Chairman, Maggie Parsons; Vice Chairman and shop, Doug Hartman; Secretary and bazaar, Joy Joy; Treasurer, Bob Butler; Covenants, Reu Brown; Membership, Val Winterflood; Christmas cards, Pauline Carmichael; Annual Draws, Peter Beaney; Collection, June Smith; Fete, Veronica James; Private Members Draw, Roy Philp; Tea Bar, Carolyn Dodd and Margaret Butcher; Project Manager, Geoff Matthews.

The committee spent much time getting to know new "local" bosses, the Horsham and

Chanctonbury Primary Care Group and further meetings were held during which the League floated the idea of a renal dialysis unit at Horsham with a planned contribution of £100,000. The PCG considered this along with a host of other new ideas including endoscopy and cataract clinics.

Trust managers pledged that all equipment purchased by the League would remain at Horsham, "except in emergencies" and this was welcomed. However it was learned with concern that some X-Ray equipment was no longer meeting required standards with the threat of a room closure whilst the era of free car parking was soon to end.

The brightest news was a gold award and £175 from Horsham in Bloom for the fine appearance of hospital gardens, a success that was to continue in years ahead with further gold, silver and bronze awards along with a special commendation from South East England in Bloom.

2000-2001: 'UNCERTAINTY' LEADS TO SPENDING EMBARGO

THE state of upheaval within health administration was reaching a height as three months of public consultation meetings were staged by West Sussex Health Authority, generating a tidal wave of protest and petitions signed by thousands of people in Horsham and Crawley.

With the future of services in the melting pot and both Maternity and Accident and Emergency due to move away from Crawley, the League in 2000 made an unprecedented step by deciding to put a freeze on major spending. This was considered to be a prudent move by the National Association which was over-seeing the closure of community hospitals across the country and, to ensure that this was within the rules, the Charity Commission was duly informed.

Bob Butler's letter spoke of "a great deal of uncertainty as to the future use of Horsham Hospital" and the decision to "hold back from paying out large sums of money on equipment" until a definite decision had been made about which services Horsham would retain and which might be transferred or discarded. The Commission replied sympathetically, pointing out the League was open to find other ways of spending its money outside the hospital.

In spite of all this a sum of £56,000 was spent that year. The committee had listened to a talk given by a back care adviser and purchased a range of manual handling equipment worth £16,737 designed to assist nurses in lifting their patients without causing back injuries. Out Patient clinics received new equipment worth £13,255, including a major item for eye testing, whilst the final bills for the Courtyard Garden were settled.

Routine annual spending had reached £8,000 covering such things as TV rentals, newspapers, fish tanks, vending machines, Christmas decorations, grants and a gift of £2,000 to Horsham mobile physiotherapy. A public telephone in Molly Andrews Way had broken, the Trust could not afford the £1,000 to replace it, so the League stepped in, paying £99 for installation and committing to quarterly rentals. Two tons of shingle costing £385 was bought to spread across gardens adjacent to the Chapel.

Fund raising went very well with a total of £79,625, another £28,392 coming from legacies and £28,131 from the League's own events. Amazingly, the tea bar produced £8,697, shop £5,457, fete £5,439, bazaar £3,965 and members draw £1,248, plus the usual contributions from collections, cards and bookstall.

At the annual meeting of May 14, 2001, tributes were paid to ambulance man John Vaughan who had died after giving 43 years work, one of the longest records of service in the country. Money devoted to his memory was spent on refurbishing courtyard gardens next to reception whilst family and friends provided a water feature along with a plaque in memory of a man much respected.

Matthew Kershaw, director of Hospital Services for Horsham and Crawley, told the meeting that the Trust was looking to enhance and develop services so that Horsham could become "a beacon of intermediate care" in the future. This was very re-assuring to all concerned and with treasurer Mr.Butler reporting assets of £292,741 there was much hope of tackling some sizeable projects in the near future.

2001-2002: NEW MANAGEMENT AND BIG SPENDING PLANS

IN the wake of decisions to move key services from Crawley to East Surrey, a major review of services across North Sussex was taking place with proposals for a new hospital at Pease Pottage at the head of the agenda. How Horsham Hospital would fit into this scenario was a matter of much speculation.

Clarity emerged with another NHS re-organisation which resulted in the PCG being magically transformed into Horsham and Chanctonbury Primary Care Trust with responsibility for doctors, dentists and chemists, a population of 102,000 people across Horsham district, management control of Horsham Hospital and a big budget.

For the first time in decades, the hospital had its own management board again, a group of experts situated locally who would decide how services would develop. At first the League was wary, however in time came to realise that this PCT would take a big interest in Horsham affairs and secure for it very substantial funding. The League was also given a place on the board, occupied by Chairman Mrs.Parsons.

The only complication was that Surrey and Sussex Trust would keep a finger in the pie by retaining control of Minor Injuries and Out Patients departments, though its Chief Executive Ken Cunningham was full of praise for the League calling it "one of the best" he had ever encountered. He also hinted that big plans for the future included new X-Ray equipment, many new clinics and more intermediate care beds.

Another remarkable year brought £136,635 income thanks mainly to five new legacies amounting to £79,759, including another property, and fund raising work of £33,485. Tea bar produced £10,769, donations and subscriptions £9,951, fete a record £7,053, shop £6,463, bazaar £4,233, private draw £1,199, cards £925, books £875, collection £804, boxes £672 and telephones £492.

At the annual meeting of May 13, 2002, Mrs.Parsons was able to report that the League had spent £360,000 on the hospital in a period of just four years, paying tribute to many supporters in all walks of life, including the town's biggest employers Sun Alliance and Novartis. Ann O'Donoghue was made a life member after working 30 years at the hospital and there were thanks also to Sally Harrison retiring after 14 years on reception.

A long list of equipment was purchased at a total cost of £72,687, the biggest item being a £37,500 Ultrasound Scanner for the fertility clinic whilst the remainder was spread across much of the hospital including an exercise system for Occupational

Therapy, chairs and tables for X-Ray, a Dinamap monitor for Minor Injuries, a Photoscanner for Out Patients, nappy changing units for Beech Community Clinic, and a myriad range of minor items.

In spite of this expenditure, the latest big surge of incoming funds resulted in a surplus on the year with assets rocketing to £349,821.

2002-2003: X-RAY SECTION IS SAVED BY BIG DONATION

IT became clear to the League that a crisis was looming in the X-Ray department. Because of ageing equipment, some of which dated back to the 1950s, more and more patients were being referred to Crawley, screening of pregnant mothers had been suspended and the knock-on effect on other departments was worrying.

With the Trust short of funds, some quick action was needed and the Friends voted in the September of 2002 to spend £170,000 on brand new equipment, redevelopment of the general room and re-opening the screening room. This decision gave X-Ray a whole new lease of life with Ken Cunningham announcing that radiology services were now secure at Horsham for many years to come. There seemed little doubt that without League intervention the days of X-Ray could have been numbered.

Whilst that work was underway, another excellent year was reported by the Treasurer with £87,943 income produced from fund raising work of £32,594, legacies £31,231, donations and subscriptions £11,490, interest £11,668 and recovered income tax of £960, derived from a covenant scheme. Assets held up at £362,831 in spite of stock market falls. The growth of tea bar work in this period was extra-ordinary, once again leading fund raising efforts with a profit of £11,392 whilst

other significant sums came from the shop £6,499, fete £5,924, bazaar £4,172, members draw £1,249, books £912, collection £763, boxes £669, cards £528 and telephones £486.

This enabled the committee to tackle several maintenance jobs which included refurbishment of bathrooms on Ash, Allcard and Oak wards at £19,277, garden and groundwork at £16,680 and more re-flooring for Leg Ulcer Clinic, John Ingham Unit and Hydropool. Two important pieces of equipment were bought for ENT at £10,433 whilst an Ocuscan Biometer for Ophthalmology costing £6,000 saved around 500 cataract patients making visits to East Surrey each year.

Certificates of merit were presented to retiring secretary Joy Joy after 13 years service, Val Winterflood who had completed 18 years on the committee and Geoff Matthews who stood down as vice chairman

At the annual meeting of May 12, 2003, Trust boss Ken Cunningham announced that transport would be organised between Horsham and Redhill to assist patients, but he believed that with coming changes the majority of people needing care could be dealt with locally.

This was supported by PCT chief Angela Ugur who revealed for the first time that the "business plan" for Horsham would involve the spending of many millions of pounds on refurbishments, expanding diagnostic work and pre-operation assessments, extra intermediate care beds for rehabilitation, improved mental health work and cover for minor injuries at weekends.

She added, however, that Horsham based mental health services would move to a new combined unit at Crawley, thus the psychiatric wing which had opened only 14 years ago as a replacement for maternity prepared for sweeping change.

CHRISTMAS AT THE HOSPITAL

PARTIES for children were a big feature at Christmas, a tradition that continued through the 1930s and 1940s, often involving more than 100 former and current patients. This event was organised by Matron Miss Horsman in 1948.

LOCAL musicians entertain on the wards.

FATHER CHRISTMAS makes an annual appearance thanks to the League, this picture with Nursing Officer Jackie Levett.

THE League provides money each year for festivities on the wards. Father Christmas is inspecting the tree on Horizon Ward in 2007 (pictured right).

2003-2004: HOSPITAL GETS £11 MILLION INVESTMENT

THE extent of new investment at Horsham was at first hard to believe, however it soon became clear that the PCT was very serious in making sure that the hospital in its care would obtain a good share of new money being poured into the NHS.

In due course, the business plan outlined by Angela Ugur was presented to Surrey and Sussex Strategic Health Authority and, much to the amazement of all concerned, a sum of £11 million was allocated for the immediate refurbishment and upgrading of Horsham Hospital.

This was the biggest slice of NHS money ever to come the way of Horsham, it brought much needed improvements to the building in general, a range of well planned new departments and a vote of confidence in the future.

League officers attended a consultation meeting with health officials at Roffey on the question of a new hospital at Pease Pottage when it became very clear that managers had no enthusiasm for the scheme recommend by the Bagnall Inquiry, preferring to see the expansion of East Surrey Hospital and the spending of what money they had on improving local services.

At the annual meeting of May 17, 2004, Ms.Ugur gave more details of the big refurbishment suggesting that Minor Injuries could be extended to seven days a week, Ante Natal work expanded along with development of a new ward for intermediate care beds and a string of new clinics. It was evident that Horsham was not going to have the benefit of a brand new hospital, but at least the existing community hospital was going to be considerably improved.

Work on upgrading X-Ray occupied much of the year with £54,000 spent on a sophisticated Siemans system and associated building works amounting to £83,650 followed by an official opening of the appropriately named Maggie Parsons Room on November 18, attended by all the top brass.

David Clark took over from treasurer Bob Butler, retiring after ten years, and could immediately report substantial income of £116,281, of which £60,230 was derived from another spate of generous legacies and £32,703 from activities. Again the tea bar was achieving miracles with profits of £13,031 whilst the book trolley run by Audrey Matthews was singled out for achieving more than £1,000. The other big sums were: shop £6,273, fete £4,831, members draw £1,240, books £1,222, collection £794, cards £664, boxes £598 and telephones £430. Assets remained at £331,171.

General spending was very modest at only £10,291, the main item being a Polaroid camera and lamp for the Dermatology Clinic at £1,257, however with £135,650 devoted to X-Ray this was still a big spending year, £147,941 in all.

2004-2005: REMARKABLE YEAR SEES £504,264 INCOME

WHAT a year this was for the League. Gross income soared to the dizzying heights of £504,264, due mainly to two substantial legacies amounting to £401,593 from the estates of Vera Frances Leach and Stanley Arnold. Their assets were released over a period of time and eventually resulted in £315,549 and £217,128 being given to the needs of the hospital.

These were breathtaking sums which transformed the shape of the League. The committee responded positively, spending £104,630 on equipment, much of which was devoted to upgrading of the Eye Clinic, whilst the unprecedented sum of £400,000 was ear-marked for the purchase of equipment needed in the big refurbishment project.

Thanks to a series of donations, the Eye Clinic had been transformed into one of the finest in the region and received much praise from surgeon Fiona O'Sullivan who said that Horsham was one of the most developed community hospitals she had visited. The latest purchases costing £45,000 were an advanced biometry machine available to patients undergoing cataract surgery and an HRT II machine designed to diagnose early stages of glaucoma, enabling many more people to be seen at Horsham.

A further £17,450 bought the very latest mole-mapping machine to assist in dealing with skin cancer, the only device of its type available within the Surrey and Sussex Trust area at that time, whilst £24,012 was devoted to an ultrasound system for vascular assessments.

With builders occupying large parts of the hospital both fete and bazaar were cancelled whilst the annual meeting of May 23, 2005, moved to the Royal Sun Alliance offices where Vice Chairman June Smith, in the Chair, unveiled the ambitious £400,000 spending programme. Long meetings with PCT officers had taken place and much sifting through equipment lists before agreement was reached for the biggest single project in the League's history.

It was agreed that the lion's share should be devoted to X-ray equipment. In 2003 the Friends had given £170,000 to replace redundant items and now they proposed a further £276,500, bringing about full modernisation of this vital department. Another favoured area was the Minor Injuries Unit for which £48,000 was made available along with a promise to buy all its new equipment.

Other sums included £10,000 for furnishing a new 12 bed unit for elderly mental health patients, £7,801 for equipping a brand new Ante-Natal Clinic, £7,343 for curtains in the new intermediate care ward, £3,000 for 14 television sets, whilst a contingency fund was retained to provide telephone services for patients and other requirements certain to arise.

Ten years of dedication to the shop came to an end with the retirement of Doug Hartman, an immensely popular worker who had taken on many other duties including organization of theatre outings for volunteers, vending machines and ward trolley, receiving in 2005 a Sussex Volunteer of the Year award. It soon became evident that a team would be needed to replace him. Chairman Mrs.Parsons was unable to continue her eleven year stint because of health problems and a rule change declared her President, only the second in the League's history following Sir Giles Loder many years previously. Certificates were presented to both Maggie Parsons and Doug Hartman for their outstanding work.

In this unique year, £76,000 was recorded under fund raising of which £29,721 was profit derived from £11,072 tea bar, £5,553 shop, £5,239 fete, £3,017 bazaar, £1,487 books, £1,301 private draw, £795 collection, £601 boxes, £579 cards and £77 telephones. More than £24,000 was also realized from subscriptions, donations and interest, whilst total assets stood at an all time record of £671,397, more than double the previous year.

LEAGUE PERSONALITIES

BOB BRUFORD joined the League on day one, February 27, 1959, and still has his original membership card, number 0026. He later served on the committee.

LONG service certificates presented to Maggie Parsons and Doug Hartman by Patron Lady Mary in 2005.

TREE planting in memory of former Chairman Maggie Parsons in October 2007 conducted by Lady Mary Mumford and Dr.David Skipp.

Speaking at the annual meeting, Angela Ugur said that the PCT had faced difficult decisions on how to spend resources, whether this should be on a new hospital or on primary care and Horsham Hospital. The decision was to concentrate on local care and with £11 million secured she believed that the 100 year-old hospital had a bright future, expressing delight that the League was contributing £400,000 which would buy approximately half of all new equipment required.

Lady Mumford rounded off a momentous meeting by saying how "wonderful" it was that Horsham had such an active League of Friends providing so much for the hospital.

2005-2006: THE ARCHITECTS OF CHANGE ARE DISBANDED

AS building work progressed, life in the hospital returned to some normality. The annual meeting of May 10, 2006, returned home, teams of volunteers, including Brownies, Guides and staff from town firms, were restoring the shape of the gardens, furniture was being steam cleaned and sparkling new departments were being phased in.

Angela Ugur spoke again of the "astounding" amount of money raised by the League, thanking members for work that had helped to make Horsham Hospital "the gem" that it was. She promised that the £400,000 was being spent well, adding that more would be done in future to secure seven days opening for Minor Injuries, more diagnostic services, more clinics and better cleanliness.

However, there was surprise news. The three year-old Horsham and Chanctonbury PCT, architects of the hospital's biggest investment and most significant period of change, were being wound up in yet another NHS re-organisation. Horsham was once more losing its locally based management.

Ms.Ugur believed that there was "one constant" at the hospital, and that was the League of Friends who would become "the focus of this hospital and the needs of the patient." The PCT was leaving the hospital in much better shape and, she hoped, "fit for another 100 years". Within a year the hospital was being run by the new West Sussex PCT based at Goring along with a new strategic health authority with responsibility for Kent, Surrey and Sussex, the South East Coast SHA.

Without a fete or a bazaar to count on, fund raising still brought in £25,540 with the tea bar recording the amazing figure of £14,560, partly put down to the hordes of workmen using the facility. Likewise the shop did very well at £6,143, books £1,458, private draw £1,035, summer draw £945, collection £753, boxes £364 and a stall in the Park £59. Until this year the League's public telephones had been making profits, however they were now recording a loss, due it was thought to the emergence of the mobile telephone.

Spending amounted to £115,983, £100,000 of which went to X-Ray as part of the big investment and £10,348 on routine services. Additional sums were devoted to equipment for Physiotherapy at £9,563 and a pachymeter for cornea eye tests at £4,425 saving 1,500 journeys a year to East Surrey and Brighton. Assets were £617,193, though with another £300,000 committed to new departments only half of that was available for future works.

The death of Doug Hartman was recorded with much sadness and a plaque on a garden bench was erected in recognition of his eleven years work, the most notable achievement being his devotion to the shop, the management of which was taken over by a team of four.

2006-2007: DISTINCTIVE NEW LOOK FOR HOSPITAL

WITH £11.4 million spent, a very different looking Horsham Hospital emerged from nearly two years of disruption. Externally the structures may not have appeared much different, however inside a revolution had occurred.

The long familiar names of Harvey, Allcard and Cope wards vanished, as did the more recently created Beech, Oak and Ash. Also gone was the operating theatre which had seen almost continuous action since 1923. Gone too was Lilac Ward in the Mental Health Unit, whilst Rose Ward was destined soon for a complete transfer to Langley Green.

The new centre-piece was The Horizon Unit, an immaculate 38 bed department standing on land once occupied by Beech and Oak, complete with modern nursing facilities for intermediate care. The area formerly occupied by Ash Ward was transformed at a cost of £1.7 million into a 12 bed unit for the Older Peoples Mental Health Service into which staff and patients from Lilac moved to inherit a new name, Iris ward.

Minor Injuries had been completely re-built and fully re-equipped by the League on a new site where Harvey ward and the operating theatre had stood, conveniently adjacent to the now totally modernised X-Ray Department that bristled with the latest equipment worth nearly £500,000, most of which had been provided by the League. The PCT had not achieved its goal of providing a seven day service at Minor Injuries, however it doubled up as the evening and week-end centre for the Out-of-Hours GP service, thereby offering medical use around the clock.

The former Beech Community Clinic was replaced by The Rainbow Unit opened in August of 2006 by Angela Ugur, a brand new building at the rear of the hospital providing for a range of outpatient services including blood testing, family planning and speech therapy, where Allcard and Cope wards once stood. A brand new Ante Natal Clinic with several new services was established in the 1923 building. The distinctive new names which had replaced the old were chosen from a PCT led competition.

League members attended a succession of official openings and were able to see at first hand what £400,000 had purchased. The last of these was the upgraded X-Ray and diagnostics section which had absorbed £276,000 of League funds, appropriately dedicated to the memory of benefactor Vera Leach with a plaque unveiled by Chairman June Smith. This money had purchased a computerised £100,000 Ultrasound Unit, Computed Radiography with Laser Imager, X-Ray equipment for the second general room, X-Ray dental equipment and £43,000 for specialist installations. It was undoubtedly one of the most impressive packages that the League had ever been associated with.

At the annual meeting of June 6, 2007, June Smith said the finished job was something that everyone in Horsham could be very proud of, adding that "patients and staff must agree that it was money well spent." There was one sad note to the proceedings following the death of President Maggie Parsons, though she had bravely managed to attend several of the opening ceremonies. There were many tributes to her devotion to the League and her campaigning for health services culminating in a tree planting ceremony in gardens adjacent to X-Ray conducted by Lady Mary and Dr.David Skipp.

MAJOR HOSPITAL FACELIFT

OPENING of the new 38 bed Horizon Unit in 2006 for which the League provided curtaining. The picture includes Angela Ugur, Maggie Parsons, Dr.Jace Clark, Barbara Wilkins and Vivienne Lyth.

THE Rainbow Unit opened by Angela Ugur in August 2006.

THE League gave £67,000 for equipping the brand new Minor Injuries Unit in 2006, opened by MP, Francis Maude pictured here with Chairman Maggie Parsons and members of staff, including Lead Nurse Barbara Dale.

It was a new era in many senses for now the hospital was being run by West Sussex PCT and Miss Smith remarked that "we are missing the close contact that we had with Horsham and Chanctonbury PCT", though looking forward with enthusiasm. There was another new name for the National Association of Friends which, after much debate became ATTEND, whilst the League joined a new body called The Community Hospital Association, a group fighting threatened closures and cutbacks.

Parking problems had always featured at annual meetings, and there was not much enthusiasm for the new pay-and-display that arrived with re-development, though volunteers were relieved to get free passes. With gardens back in shape again it was decided to enter Horsham in Bloom once more but, in spite of all that had been achieved, League membership had slipped below 1,000 for the first time in many years and efforts were made to seek new support. It was pointed out that membership cost only £1 per year.

Sue Giddings of West Sussex PCT outlined future policy to provide services close to people's homes. A "huge amount" had been achieved at Horsham, she went on, and the new Horizon Unit was making a tremendous impact towards that goal.

The balance sheet made fascinating reading. Spending in the year came to an all-time record £419,856, of which £300,000 was the balance for new departments, revised as follows: four pieces of sophisticated X-Ray equipment £170,177; Minor Injuries equipment £67,601; Iris Ward £30,528; curtains for the Horizon Unit £11,560; Ante Natal £6,337 and a further £13,899 on miscellaneous items. With the £100,000 spent in X-Ray a year previously that extraordinary list accounted for the League's promised £400,000.

A sum of £5,897 went on regular services whilst there was still time to spend another £57,000 on other important items including a retinal camera for the Eye Clinic, a revolutionary portable Ultrasound system for the speedy checking of damage to soft tissues and Hopps sensory equipment. Smaller buys included scales, wheelchairs, new vending machines, pool table repair for Rose Ward and training for staff in the Falls Clinic.

With both fete and bazaar revived, there was healthy income of £29,297 from activities, £26,870 subscriptions and donations and £23,451 interest. The tea bar again topped the fund-raising league with £14,107 followed by shop £5,669, fete £3,250, bazaar £1,857, bookstall £1,524, private draw £1,150, cards £719, collection £697 and boxes £616.

Treasurer David Clark reported the League in a healthy state with £330,000 of assets available for further major projects.

2007-2008: TRIBUTES TO FOUNDING INSPIRATION

THE life of Molly Andrews, who died aged 88 in May, 2008, was fondly remembered at the League's annual meeting. Molly had served as hospital administrator for 36 years, was a considerable inspiration in the founding of the League of Friends in 1959 and was one of its proudest supporters.

She began work there in 1944 before the arrival of the NHS, was a driving force behind major expansion of the 1970s, Chairman June Smith calling her "a model of efficiency and kindness which resulted in a happy hospital." The significance of her impact remains etched into one of the main corridors still known as Molly Andrews Way. Not even the 2005 refurbishment would erase that.

Because hospital space was now very limited, the 49th annual meeting on June 11 was moved to the Salvation Army Hall where Miss Smith said that the League was once more adapting to change and coming to terms with new structures which had merged five local PCTs into one that served the whole county. Senior officers of West Sussex PCT gave a talk on the future of primary care and community nursing whilst members were introduced to the new head of Community Hospital Services, Clare Loft, now responsible for Horsham.

There were tributes to several long serving volunteers who had each devoted many years to the tea bar including Joyce Tickner, 25 years, and Joy Lewis, 20 years. A bouquet was presented to Mrs.Mary Phillips whose hand-made dolls house had raised a sum of £1,000 and praise too for volunteers who had achieved a silver medal from the latest Horsham in Bloom contest. There was amazement that the book trolley in reception had raised a record £2,348.

Fund raising work had not slackened at all. Interest accounted for £22,175, subscriptions and donations brought in £13,618 whilst activities produced the grand sum of £31,978. Among several donations was a sum of £400 raised by pensioner Joan Lockyer through opening her garden to visitors each summer.

Tea bar profits topped the league now every year and the full list was: tea bar £13,856, shop £6,405, fete £3,713, books £2,348, bazaar £2,745, private draw £1,162, cards £1,017, collection £659, boxes £627. The fete had been boosted by £985 from the dolls house draw and the regular summer draw which contributed £1,278. Likewise, draw tickets had complemented takings from the bazaar stalls with a sum of £1,376.

It was not surprising, perhaps, that after all the huge decisions of the previous few years, 2007 was to prove one of the lowest for expenditure in many years. In all, just £19,641 was donated, £13,906 on equipment and regular services, the largest item being an Axis Shield for the Warfarin Clinic, with £5,735 taken up by general running expenses.

However, the League had emerged from a three year period which had seen spending of an unprecedented scale and a hospital with a positive future.

2008-2009: LEAGUE'S £2 MILLION CONTRIBUTION

AS the League began the 50th year, it was possible to ascertain the full extent of its contribution to Horsham Hospital during that half century. The recorded accounts show that total spending on equipment and amenities came to £2,140,000. By any standards, an amazing achievement.

The rate of spending accelerated with the passing years. During the first 25 the sum of £140,367 had been spent whilst in the last four alone the figure came to £705,479.

Biggest sum in any year was the £400,000 given during the 2005 refurbishment, divided amongst several departments. In 1997 £225,000 was devoted to equipping the new Out Patients whilst the League can claim to have completely modernised the X-Ray Department over a period of years, fully equipped Minor Injuries and made a very significant contribution towards establishing a top class Eye Clinic.

During 2008 requests for new equipment emerged from all directions and it became obvious too that the PCT was in need of more help in sustaining good maintenance.

By the middle of the year the committee had identified a string of projects which would require at least £150,000, the biggest of which was the urgently needed modernisation of public toilets in Molly

Andrews Way, something the League had pressed for many years, originally to be paid for by the NHS, but now financed by the League at an estimated £50,000.

This work would mean the League losing part of its small store-room and a solution was found when the PCT agreed to give up a portion of the kitchen area for conversion. The League happily grabbed this opportunity, spending £14,000 to provide space for equipment and stocks associated with fete and bazaar plus a new archive area in which records and rare surviving documents were deposited. The store-room fulfilled a long discussed need for extra space.

Other significant sums were spent on 21 items of equipment spread across many different parts of the hospital including X-Ray, Child Development Clinic, Physiotherapy, Horizon Unit, Hydrotherapy, Out Patients, Main Reception, Minor Injuries, Opthalmology, Diabetic Clinic and Podiatry. The biggest of these was £17,000 for a cardiac investigation kit, £17,000 towards an OCT machine to further boost the Eye Clinic, 36 chairs for Physiotherapy and new blinds for Horizon.

Further money was needed to purchase a new boiler for the ever popular tea bar, though this was not all surprising because the numbers of teas being provided had rocketed in the previous five years, producing record profits but placing great strain on the facilities.

It was decided to give the summer fete a new look with a range of additional family attractions whilst the appearance of Lord Tebbit to perform the opening attracted a big crowd on a warm and sunny day. In his address, the famous Tory peer stressed the vital importance of Horsham Hospital in an ever-changing NHS structure and was full of praise for staff, rescue services and the League. The day resulted in a bright start to fund raising with proceeds of around £6,600, of which £3,286 came from a highly successful prize draw.

The pre-occupation of West Sussex PCT was their "Fit For The Future" consultation on future services at Haywards Heath, Worthing and Chichester to which the League offered its own observations, once again raising the question of how the new management proposed to deal with patients in North Sussex. The outcome was another review covering Horsham and Crawley undertaken by Sir Graeme Catto though, unlike the earlier Bagnall Inquiry, his remit did not include the continuing call for a new hospital at Pease Pottage.

Further changes at the hospital took place late in 2008 with the transfer of the 29 bed Rose Ward from the Mental Health Unit to the brand new £16 million Langley Green Hospital. Some mental health services, including the Lavender day unit, were remaining though the wheelchair centre was taking over part of the former Mental Health building to make way for another refurbishment of the ever faithful 1892 premises now facing a new future as an administrative centre.

The Christmas bazaar was cancelled to make way for a special celebration party marking the League's 50th anniversary on February 27, 2009, followed by a concert given by the Slinfold Silver Band in April.

In the 50th year the shape of the committee was thus: Chairman, June Smith; Vice Chairman, David Briffett; Secretary, Sue Martin; Treasurer, David Clark; Gift Aid, Reu Brown; Membership, Valerie Winterflood; Christmas cards, Pauline Carmichael; Summer and Christmas draws, Peter Beaney; Private Members Draw, Maureen Francis; Tea Bar, Margaret Butcher and Carolyn Dodd; Shop, Bryan Thompson, Albert Marrable, Elsie Lee, Ken Clark; Gardens, Lilian Bold.

Whilst these 16 people shoulder much of the organisation, the League of Friends itself is a much bigger entity that could not function at all without the involvement of many others.

The membership, currently 964, provides a very substantial element of support by paying subscriptions and participating in regular events. There are more than 120 volunteers who work in the tea bar and shop through a rota system and whose presence raises thousands of pounds each year.

Teams of volunteers help keep the gardens in shape. Numerous individuals give help in dozens of different ways including members of staff, retired staff, doctors and especially the porters.

Other tremendous support is received from tradesmen, the town's employers, local authorities, community groups, fund raisers of all shapes and sizes, all of whom clearly have a corner in their heart for the local hospital.

Without them there would be no League of Friends and Horsham Hospital would not be quite the same place that it is today.

COMMITTEE MEMBERS

THE League's 49th annual meeting in June, 2008, attended by Chairman of Horsham District Council John Bailey, with committee members Pauline Carmichael, Peter Beaney, Reu Brown, Lady Mary Mumford, Val Winterflood, Maureen Francis, June Smith and David Clark.

**A COMMITTEE meeting in 2001.
Back row,
Carolyn Dodd,
Vera Meadows,
Doug Hartman,
Pauline Carmichael,
Val Winterflood,
Reu Brown,
Geoff Matthews.
Front row,
June Smith,
Bob Butler,
Maggie Parsons,
Joy Joy and
Margaret Butcher.**